W9-DFE-286

CONTEMPORARY JEWISH
CIVILIZATION SERIES

In cooperation with
Institute of Contemporary Jewry,
Hebrew University of Jerusalem

MOSHE DAVIS, Editor

OTHER VOLUMES IN THIS SERIES:

Yehuda Bauer, *Flight and Rescue: Brichah*

Simon N. Herman, *Israelis and Jews*

Moshe Davis, *The Changing Jewish People*
(to be published in 1973)

Tradition and Reality

The Impact of History
on Modern Jewish Thought

TRADITION
and
REALITY

The Impact of History on Modern Jewish Thought

by Nathan Rotenstreich

RANDOM HOUSE  NEW YORK

WITHDRAWN
Burlington, Vermont

19700

BM
195
.R84

Copyright © 1972 by Nathan Rotenstreich

All rights reserved under International
and Pan-American Copyright Conventions.
Published in the United States by Random House, Inc.,
New York, and simultaneously in Canada
by Random House of Canada Limited, Toronto.

ISBN: 0-394-46425-7

Library of Congress Catalog Card Number: 71-159369

Manufactured in the United States of America

9 8 7 6 5 4 3 2
First Edition

FOR GERSCHOM SCHOLEM

Master and Source of Inspiration

AUTHOR'S NOTE

THIS BOOK IS AN ATTEMPT to reveal the contemporary mind of the Jews insofar as it is shaped by attitude to tradition. The methodical assumption is that the contemporary Jewish mind is a conglomerate of different intellectual trends, stemming from a crisis in Jewish history which originated in the nineteenth century and has continued into our own time. The core of this crisis seems to lie in the emergence of a historical consciousness among Jews and, particularly, in the application of that consciousness to their own tradition and the norms inherent in it. The task I set for myself is to trace and analyze the salient phases through which their attitude to tradition and its binding quality passed as a result. Though my main concern in this book is the mind of the present, I assume that, knowingly or unknowingly, this mind of the present has been shaped by individual thinkers whose teachings continue to influence opinion and behavior.

I wish to thank Professor Moshe Davis, Head of the Institute of Contemporary Jewry of the Hebrew University of Jerusalem for the suggestion to write this book and Max Gartenberg and Alice Mayhew for their work in editing the manuscript. Mrs.

Grabriele Schalit, who helped me prepare the index and glossary, has also deserved my gratitude. Mrs. Saphir-Braun worked with me on the manuscript and helped me greatly.

I should here also express my appreciation for the assistance provided me by the Memorial Foundation for Jewish Culture.

The Lucius N. Littauer Foundation and its distinguished president, Mr. Harry Starr, have helped me not only in the preparation of the present book but in my study of the history of Jewish ideas over the years. I am deeply grateful to them for their continuing interest and support.

N. R.

Jerusalem, 1972

CONTENTS

PART ONE

Background

INTRODUCTION

THE THEME OF THIS BOOK is the fundamental shift that has taken place in modern Jewish consciousness—in the attitudes towards their past and towards tradition held by the generations of Jews since the early nineteenth century.

The far-reaching intellectual, emotional and social consequences of this change for Jews, individually and collectively, can be understood only when we take into account the religious character of the Jewish past and the consequent demand that traditions and values be observed with binding constancy. A religion based on revelation which took place in the past requires subjection of the now to what has come before; it sets boundaries to creativity; it assumes that there is no room for independent formulation except for commentary and elaboration on the given body of truth.

Once Jews were granted political and legal rights and became involved in the cultures of their environments, tradition no longer filled the whole scope of their lives. No longer excluded from the mainstream of world history, they began to live simultaneously in the Jewish and non-Jewish environments. The fixed system of religious norms was shaken by the impact of the modern historical sense. For over a thousand years "the vital and exciting 'action' was not in the Bible, but in the Bible commentary. It was there that you made your discoveries and defined yourself and your values."[1] In the nineteenth century commentary gave way to research. Tradition itself became the subject matter of historical, literary and philological examination according to the standards and concepts prevailing in modern scholarship. A process of what may be called de-sacration was implicit in this attempt towards objective examination and study.

How did Jews react to the introduction of historic relativism into the discourse of their generations? Since the tradition might now be seen as no longer having the binding character of the supra-historical, there were Jews who refused to be bound by it on historical grounds. They rejected any sense of attachment to Jewish history and would not recognize the Jews as an ethnic entity. The other response has been to see the Jewish tradition as historical, part of the evolution in time of the Jewish people. The result would then be the emancipation of Jewish peoplehood from its immersion in religion and tradition. But a people, being at least partially defined as a historic entity, cannot evade the question of its relation to the past. Tradition, though no longer the sole imperative, remains a factor in the present.

What happens when the authority of a millennial tradition begins to erode, is not easy to describe. Liberation from the past takes place in time; it does not follow a straight and easily discernible line. The stages in the process are at the same time components of the mind of the present.

Thus, for example, the nineteenth-century philosopher of history, Nachman Krochmal, tried to find a synthesis between the eternal position and the historical transformations of the Jewish people. His solution was a cyclical concept of Jewish history. This concept, in popular formulation, is not uncommon among Jews today, who, having experienced both the Holocaust and the restoration of the Jewish Commonwealth, see the first as representing a period of decline in the cycle and the second a period of resurgence. There is no conscious dependence on Krochmal here, yet Krochmal's teachings appear as factors in an evolving Jewish consciousness.

In the following pages we shall consider such thinkers as Krochmal, such historians as Graetz and Dubnow, and the founders of the "Science of Judaism," who shaped modern Jewish research and historical consciousness. They were followed by others, like Ahad Ha-am and Bialik, who, against the new background of modern Zionism and the national renaissance, tried to come to grips with the relation between past and present. All these men gave expression to the erosion of traditional Jewish consciousness and in so doing gave, as a matter of fact, additional momentum to the process.[2] Indeed, the establishment of the State of Israel itself has aggravated, rather than resolved, the problem. For the new commonwealth involves Jews in a diversity of social, economic and political experiences and activities which go beyond the boundaries of traditional concepts.

Clearly, the shift from one period of history to another has not removed the problem. It has only placed it on a new level.

CHAPTER ONE

The Meaning of Tradition in Judaism

IN ORDER TO COMPREHEND the meaning and significance of "tradition" in Judaism, three of the principal definitions generally given to the word must be distinguished.

The first meaning of tradition (*Massoret*) refers to the faithful, word-for-word carrying over of the text of the Bible, the punctuation, dotting, accents, syntax, etc., unchanged and unamended. Tradition in this sense is a documentary and textual discipline.

The second meaning of tradition refers to the whole domain of religious writing in its theoretical and legal aspects. This body of work is essentially Biblical interpretation, comprising a running commentary on the Scriptures. In trying to establish a connection between the first and second meanings of tradition, the nineteenth-century Christian philosopher F. J. Molitor declared that the first refers to the external aspect of the word of the Bible and the second to its internal aspect, that is, its content.[1]

This distinction, however, does not do full justice to the complexity of the subject. To separate content from the words in which it is expressed is to fail to recognize the dialectic of tradition inherent in its textual and its legal-theological aspects. It is only through interpretation, after all, that the words of the text receive their meaning, significance and value. On the other hand, however, the second meaning of tradition implies the basic assumption of Judaism—and here there is no fundamental difference between Judaism and the other positive religions— that the literary document is actually the basis of religious life. A religious value is thus assigned to tradition in its purely textual aspect, and the interpretation of content is intimately connected with a strict regard for words. To put this another way, tradition extended its meaning from the sphere of words to the sphere of content when religious life struck roots in the text and became inseparably conjoined with it.

These two meanings, however, do not exhaust the idea of tradition. With the introduction of a third meaning we leave the realms of literary production and theoretical thinking and enter into historical reality—specifically, the history of a group or people.

In this third meaning, tradition comprises the totality of life as shaped and handed down from generation to generation. The transition from the first two meanings of tradition to the third is again connected with the very nature of Judaism. Since the literary document is not merely theoretical but the very fabric of the social life of the community, the text itself constitutes an essential factor in the historical continuity of the people. In other words, the content of the Bible entails obligations in the practical conduct of the individual and the community; and as such conduct touches on the sphere of history, a necessary relation is established among text, interpretation and the history of the society. Although the three meanings of tradition become manifest in the course of Jewish history, their interrelation is not merely historical but also systematic, involving a number of problems which we will have to consider.

From the point of view of the development of modern Jewish thought, it is principally the second and third meanings of tradition—namely, the interpretation which reveals content and the people's actual experience in relation to a literary document—that concern us most. And from this viewpoint, it will be instructive to see how these two meanings were approached from two intellectual extremes, that of the Middle Ages and that of the nineteenth century.

In his Introduction to *Hovath Ha-Levavoth,* Bahya ibn Pakuda (ca. 1080) states that there are three gates to the knowledge of God: (1) sound reason; (2) the books of the Torah given to Moses; and (3) the traditions handed down from our ancestors who received them from the Prophets.[2] Here Bahya presents the three sources of religious knowledge—reason, revelation and tradition—as coexistent and complementary. Bahya does not analyze their interrelations, although he understood that tradition, as a source of religious knowledge, appeared at a stage of religious life subsequent to revelation. The sequence in time of revelation and tradition did not influence Bahya's opinion as to the reliability of tradition as a legitimate source of religious knowledge.

The secondary character of tradition, which received scant attention in the Middle Ages, became an increasingly important element in the philosophical and historical thought of later centuries, and a central problem in the nineteenth century. If revelation comes first and tradition second, obviously the latter becomes derivative and secondary. But the secondariness of tradition is offset by the fact that tradition is the avenue to the meaning of revelation, which must be re-interpreted continually according to the changing spirit of the times. To put this in the language of values: the value of revelation lies in its status as the original and primary stage of religious consciousness, while the value of tradition is derived from its being the advanced stage of progress of that consciousness. But there is now a tension between tradition and revelation which did not appear in the Middle Ages, when these two sources of religious knowledge were thought of as existing side by side.

This tension is apparent in Abraham Geiger's attempt, formulated against the background of the nineteenth century, to distinguish four periods in Jewish history. These were: (1) the period of revelation, which coincides with the Biblical era; (2) the Talmudic period; (3) the period from the completion of the Talmud up to the eighteenth century; and (4) the period from the eighteenth century onward, described as the period of criticism. The three post-Biblical periods were characterized by Geiger as governed by tradition,[3] and it is evident that in each succeeding traditional period the original revelation becomes increasingly remote.

Solomon Formstecher, a contemporary of Geiger, posited three stages in the development of Jewish religious consciousness: revelation, prophecy and tradition. In prophecy the word of God, being the principle of religious creativity, still appears in its living relation to man, whereas in tradition it appears as a datum expressed either in the Torah or in the books of the Prophets. Tradition, according to Formstecher, connotes reflection applied to the word of God as datum. It would appear then that the first two stages of religious consciousness constitute a more authoritative source than the third, since they are founded on a vivid and direct contact with God's word. But to Formstecher this is not the whole case. Although it may be less reliable in the religious sense than revelation or prophecy, tradition includes a factor lacking in the former two—that is, human creativity. Formstecher thus links the first two stages together in what he calls the period of religious objectivity to distinguish them from the third stage, which comprises the period of religious subjectivity. In the earlier period of Jewish history the medium of religious knowledge is the immediate apprehension of the word of God, and its literary expression is prophecy. In the modern period the medium of religious knowledge is reason, and its typical expression and formative force is tradition.

Here we find a clear expression of the tension already alluded to. Tradition, the source of religious knowledge in Judaism which appears later in time, becomes distinctive in its subjectivity, and subjectivity now appears as the very principle of religious consciousness and content. From this standpoint the Talmud could be considered superior to the Bible because, being a creation of the third stage, it is rooted in reflection. But here the philosophy of history and theory of knowledge in the modernistic trends of Jewish thought came into conflict with their own evaluations of Judaism's fundamental documents. Although it seemed logical to do so, it was not possible to assign inferior status to the Bible as an earlier document in comparison with the Talmud as a later document. The contradiction nevertheless opened a path towards understanding tradition and assessing its epistemological and religious status.[4]

THE RELATION BETWEEN REVELATION AND TRADITION can also be formulated as a transition from the metaphysical-transcendent to the historical-immanent sphere. This transition has two aspects, time and content. Revelation is a finite occurrence from the standpoint of man; it takes place in historical time, which as such can be determined. From God's standpoint, however, revelation in an atemporal occurrence. Thus in the very essence of revelation we meet a fundamental contradiction.

The transition in time, moreover, is accompanied by a transition in content, since revelation is contained and implied in tradition. Revelation serves with respect to tradition both as origin and reservoir of the contents to be cultivated and developed. On the one hand, tradition is the immediate link after revelation; on the other, it is its interpretation. The interdependence of revelation and tradition is constant and ongoing: revelation without tradition is undefined; tradition without revelation is void of meaning. Yet tradition is essentially historical and revelation essentially supra-historical. Their relationship is aptly expressed in the Catholic description of revelation as the *caput et origo* of tradition.

But here we encounter another problem as well. Revelation as a divine act forms a link in the chain of history, that is, a link in tradition. Revelation is therefore not only the content which serves as a basis for history but also the initial or founding event in the continuing historical process. Thus revelation creates history through its content and through its dependence upon God who reveals himself in it. But only the content of revelation enters into the continuity of tradition, while the act or event of revelation itself remains transcendent against that continuity. Professor Gershom Scholem explains the relation between tradition and revelation in this way: "In Judaism tradition becomes the reflective moment which plants itself between the Absolute of the divine word, which is revelation, and its receiver."[5]

In classical Roman Catholic thought, the relationship is defined in two ways. From a substantive point of view revelation and tradition are regarded by the Church as completely identical, tradition being held to be only a conservation of the revealed content. In spite of this identity, a formal distinction is made between tradition and revelation: the former is a matter of the Church on behalf of God, the latter of God alone.[6] This distinction, however, leaves out the aspect of modality: that is, revelation is in the sphere of the absolute, while tradition is in the sphere of relations, including the relation with the sphere of the absolute. Hence the primary problem of religious consciousness entails a perplexity: how does the sphere of the absolute establish the sphere of relativity, and how can the lines between the spheres of the absolute and relativity be determined?

IN ATTEMPTING TO ANSWER THESE QUESTIONS, we may consider the relation between the two spheres as one of opposite vectors. It is possible in this light to understand the well-known dictum of Yehuda Halevi that the public character of the revelation on Mount Sinai is evidence of its reliability. The very statement points to a dialectic paradox. Tradition—the record of the revelation on Mount Sinai—is presented as evidence of the revelation itself. Without tradition there is no intersubjective information to confirm that the revelation took place; or to put it differently, tradition, whose foundation is revelation, is nevertheless the medium that conveys our knowledge of it. From the ontological and material point of view, tradition is bound up with revelation, but from the point of view of consciousness revelation is bound to tradition. Furthermore, the content of revelation is the content of traditional (that is, historical) consciousness.

But this consciousness assumes its content not as its own but as given to it by revelation. When the historical consciousness of tradition is not aware of its dependence upon the dimension beyond it, the distinction between transcendence and immanence tends to become attenuated or obliterated, as occurs when the religious content is identified with the substance of history. We meet such a tendency in the thought of the nineteenth-century philosopher of history Nachman Krochmal, who regarded the Absolute Spirit as the substance of the history of the Jewish people, that is, as the people's national spirit. But genuine religious consciousness has only one way open to it, namely, perpetuating the tension between an absorption in revealed content and a realization of the absence of sovereignty over that content.

We can therefore understand two opposed solutions to the problem of the relationship between revelation and tradition which appear in Judaism. The mystical or "ecstatic" solution seeks to abolish normal consciousness, for consciousness absorbed in a transcendent content has no position of its own. The mystic attempts to pitch his consciousness on the level of the substance of content—in God rather than the word of God. Content is never a part of consciousness, and never ceases to be of overriding validity. The polarity between consciousness and content is thus resolved by the submergence of the former in the latter.

There is, on the other hand, the concept of created reason,

elaborated in the modern Jewish philosophy of Hermann Cohen. According to this view, functional consciousness is permeated with the content of revelation. The created consciousness is thus related — or correlated[7] — to the revealed content. Since it was created by the Revealer himself, consciousness becomes an integral part of the revelatory process, and a way is opened for meaningful, continuous exposition.

WITHIN THE SPHERE OF JUDAISM a further connection must be pointed out, a connection which cannot be deduced from the formal status of the idea of tradition. The historical community, the Jewish people, as a community living its life in time, becomes both the substance for the materialization of commandments and an active agent in that materialization. In this conception of Judaism a distinction can hardly be made between the two modes of relationship pointed out by Schleiermacher, namely, whether religion is society or whether religion has society as a substratum.[8] The community which was made the substratum for norms thus becomes a norm in itself, and the life of the community becomes integrated in the sphere of faith. From this integration a number of conclusions may be derived regarding the third meaning of tradition, not as the principle of religious consciousness but as the totality of life.

Through this connection with the community, the idea of tradition became not merely a principle constituting the historical consciousness of the Jews but also an idea that created and fostered their historical reality. It may be of some interest here to note the difference between the idea of tradition in Judaism and the classical idea of tradition in Roman Catholicism. Tradition in Roman Catholicism, bound to the sphere of dogmatic and theoretic statements of the Church and also to its hierarchical structure, is composed of the theoretical and institutional aspects of the life of the Church. It is in essence an attempt to combine the demand for an authoritative interpretation of the dogma with the demand for a hierarchical administration of the Church throughout the generations. Tradition in its Roman Catholic sense does not comprehend the full totality of the life of communities, because Catholicism represents for these communities a dogmatic and institutional system brought to them from the outside. Therefore, we find in Catholicism the need for stressing the formal characteristic of tradition, such as *universalitas, antiquitas, consensus omnium.* In the idea of tradition in Judaism, however, the totality of life is involved, and tradition is limited neither to its dogmatic nor to its institutional aspect. The life of Jewish society constitutes the very content of tradition. It is determined by tradition in its theoretical meaning but, at the same time, passes beyond the sphere of theory or doctrine. Tradition in its theoretical formulation appears in fact as the historical consciousness of the Jewish community, a consciousness that creates and reflects the history of that community. Thus tradition necessarily involves the tension between the sphere of meaning and consciousness, on the one hand, and the sphere of actual history and life time on the other. Through this integration, tradition as a norm of life becomes involved in the historical life and complex problems of the community.

In this third, or social, meaning, tradition is called upon to solve problems in the relations between the generations. The idea of tradition as a totality of the actual life of a community is based on two assumptions: that there is a transmitting and a receiving generation but that the creative expressions of the receiving generation are concordant with the meanings and norms contained in the legacy of the transmitting generation. Moreover, all the generations are enveloped in an absolute sphere of values which determines their internal relations beyond their relationships in time, so that the temporal differences between generations do not affect their common adherence to the legacy. The idea of tradition in this sense identifies historical reality with a specific meaning, that is, the word of God. It rejects the view that a transition from the sphere of meaning to that of everyday life implies a change in meaning or a change in reality. [9]

The outlook based in tradition considers history as a synthesis between meaning and reality. Without this synthesis there is no sense in the relation between the generations based on a religious, ethical or theoretical norm. But in this synthesis the determining factor is that of meaning; reality is a datum and does not in itself possess the factors which shape it and constitute its content. It is merely the substratum for the materialization of meaning.

The relation between the two factors establishing historical reality—time and meaning—is one-sided: from meaning to time. In other words, it is not only the historical consciousness of the generations which is fashioned by the religious content—consciousness being only the conservation of this content—but historical reality is itself established by the content. Tradition in its theoretical meaning is the content of the generations' consciousness and also the causative force that creates their reality. History thus is condensed into meaning. As causative force, tradition presupposes a correlation between the generations: the transmitted content is not innate or indigenous to a generation but merely given in the word of God. The legacy is both imposed and willingly identified with by the successive generations.

As a result of such identification, the generations become ideally absorbed in the legacy. The present historical experience of every generation calls for its identification with the past. The dimension of the past becomes the decisive-normative one; in fact, it is the only dimension in the concept of time inherent in tradition, if we leave out of account the future as the dimension of redemption or messianic salvation. For, following the formula of Saint Augustine, we may say that from the traditional viewpoint the present is always the presence of the past but the past has an independent status and is only the past in regard to the present. The factual existence of the present is thus not an independent existence in the sphere of meaning. From the point of view of reality the present exists independently, but from the perspective of meaning the present is an offshoot only. This concept of the dimensions of historical time mirrors the religious view of history which holds the past to be superior to the present. But the significance of the past as the reservoir of content is not a historical one; its validity is based on its relation to the absolute content of revelation.

Thus we can understand the philosophical significance of an important turn in Jewish history — the crisis of secularization. Secularization is an attempt to detach the reality of everyday life from its integration in the determined and determining meaning of tradition by the creation of a new meaning. It seeks to elevate the present from an offshoot to an autonomous division of time, to the level of an independent causative factor.

How, we may ask, is this attribution of meaning to present reality possible? To answer the question we must distinguish between tradition as the totality of life and tradition as historical consciousness. The connection of the generations with one content and the identity of that content over the generations establishes continuity. But tradition is, in fact, cumulative; the actual reality of a people comprises a body of contents which appear in the course of history through their relation to the *one* content. In addition to being cumulative, tradition is also selective. A historical concept of tradition has to come to terms with differences of opinion in Jewish history and with the facts of different and clashing movements and trends. All of these divergences are aspects of tradition, but decisions made with respect to them have been historical rather than dogmatic. The practical problem in tradition is thus that of the relationship between accumulation and selection: how to justify selection within the scope of an accumulated totality. So factors of value and meaning are introduced into history, and these inhere in the present rather than come from the past.

With the secularization of Jewish life beginning in the nineteenth century, the process of selection became a challenging and unremitting one. If Judaism was to be preserved, then by what means? And what aspects of Judaism were relevant to the changing autonomous present? The answers were of several kinds, as can be seen in an examination of the chief trends of thought and representative thinkers on the problem of tradition and reality.

PART TWO

History
Against Norms

CHAPTER TWO

The Science of Judaism

IN THE COURSE OF THE NINETEENTH CENTURY a movement emerged which became known as *Wissenschaft des Judentums* or the "Science of Judaism." The manifestation of this movement is a confluence of scholarly, historical and philological investigations summed up in articles and books concerning various aspects of Judaism and the Jewish people. Yet underlying this scholarly output is a definite ideology, and one which has left its stamp on Jewish thought in modern times.

THE DOMINANT FIGURE in the Science of Judaism is Leopold Zunz, who was born in Detmold, Germany, in 1794. In 1817, when he was still a student in the University of Berlin, Zunz wrote an article "On Rabbinical Literature." In it he argued for the recognition of Jewish literature and religion as subjects for university research and instruction, pointing out their connection with other disciplines and their consequent place in the history of these disciplines. "Here," he wrote, "the whole literature of the Jews, in its largest scope, is put forward as subject matter for research, without concern as to whether its total content ought and can be also the norm for our own evaluation."[1]

The importance of this work cannot be overestimated. It struck so responsive a chord in the world of younger Jewish scholars and intellectuals that within a year of its publication in 1818, Zunz together with Eduard Gans and Moses Moser was able to found a Society for the Culture and Science of Judaism, whose expressed aim was "to bring the Jews into harmonious relations with the age and the nations in which they live." The society attracted some of the brightest Jewish youths of Germany — Heinrich Heine was for a time a member — and even published a magazine which Zunz edited. Although the group dissolved after a few years, its ideals continued to spread throughout Europe and new centers of the Science of Judaism sprang up in France and Galicia as well as in Germany, continuing into the twentieth century.*

FOR ALL THE EXCITEMENT it stirred, the Science of Judaism was a rather austere discipline and not a religious revival in any sense. It was not interested in preserving the continuity of Judaism. Neither was it part of any effort directed at liberating Judaism from dependence on traditional values and forms. Nor did it stem from a desire to *acquire* objectivity by the extinction of feelings of involvement or commitment. It was based instead on the assumption that the severance of all connections with the world of tradition was an accomplished, incontrovertible fact. The purpose of the Science of Judaism was not to restore that world but, by close study, to understand it.

This is entirely different from the many endeavors to interpret Judaism, its traditions, laws, customs and habits whose purpose was to make plainer to the people the intent and meaning of

---

* The Science of Judaism underwent significant changes as it developed. In this study, we shall be concerned only with the founding generation, whose programs and ideas are particularly relevant to our subject.

their heritage. On the contrary, these selfsame endeavors became material to be studied under the Science of Judaism with detachment and without regard to the feelings they might arouse.

This scientific or conceptual attitude owed much to Hegel, who likened philosophy to the owl of Minerva, which made its appearance only in the evening, after the sun had set. By its very nature, conceptual thinking adds nothing new to its object, and the Science of Judaism offered nothing substantive. Its principal function was to discern the given and to elevate it to the level of the known, specifically to understand Judaism in its proper context and to determine its place in human cultural evolution. Furthermore, the special mark of this approach lay in its assumption that the chain of creativity had been broken, the source of inspiration had dried up, and the previous, living body of Judaism had been laid to rest.[2] The Science of Judaism did not derive its historical perspective from the feeling that it was introducing changes into the world of Judaism, but from a consciousness of the distance between that world and itself.

THIS ATTITUDE OF DETACHMENT toward the accomplishments of the Jewish past achieved further expression in a desire for liberation from theological preconceptions. First and foremost among these was the Christian view of Jewish creativity, and especially its literary documents, as material either of service to the Church or opposed and inimical to it.[3] Post-Biblical Jewish literature, which by right should have been acknowledged as an independent field and appraised by criteria distinctive to Judaism, was denied an intrinsic value by the Church. The Church's position that this literature was merely symbolic represented a distortion, according to the view of the Science of Judaism. The proponents of the Science recognized post-Biblical Judaism as possessing independent value, which could be understood on its own terms without being tied to preconceptions or measured by external criteria.

The very rejection of the Christian theological view, however, carried with it a rejection of any normative status for Judaism, that is, one in which the past of Judaism might serve as a guide or outline to the present. The research attitude which regards every detail as important in defining the overall pattern was to be carefully distinguished from that subservience which regards every detail as holy.[4] Later in the century, when the Science of Judaism became a part of the movement for Jewish national revival, the past was reconsidered in terms of its value to the present, but this had no place in the original program of Zunz and his colleagues.

THE DETACHMENT upon which the Science of Judaism was based was, in fact, diametrically opposed to all forms of romanticism. The Science of Judaism did not embrace the past as an escape from the present, extolling it for its superior virtues. On the contrary, it openly declared its disengagement from the past, placing itself at a distance from the past in order to maintain its objective, conceptual attitude.[5] In this respect, it differed from the so-called German Historical School, which also studied the past conceptually but regarded it as a force guiding the present. The Historical School did not arrogate to itself the right to sever historical relationships with the past; it rejected any attempt arising out of a present awakening and initiative to act freely and independently, since such action would, specifically, break with the past. The achievements of the past were a manifestation of *Volksgeist,* or "The Spirit of the People," of which the creativity of the present was an organic outgrowth. Thus to the Historical School the concern with the past was limited by a subjective, and even selective, principle. The Science of Judaism, on the other hand, started out from and endeavored to maintain a total objectivity.[6]

This attitude extended to the very heart of Judaism, the realm of values. It was an indisputable premise of the Science of

Judaism that literary documents existed which revealed certain states of mind, that these documents could be examined, and that the states of mind could be learned from them. In addition, particular people and circumstances were involved in the production of each document and their involvement was to be accepted as an empirical fact. The works might be studied for their content, for their literary quality or for what they revealed about the human societies which produced them, according to the historian and friend of Zunz, Isaac Marcus Jost, but not to prove the virtues or shortcomings of Judaism.[7] The only values of relevance to the Science of Judaism must be scientific values.

In their examination of the present, as well as the past, the founders of the Science of Judaism maintained the same detachment, focusing their attention on the examination of literary and linguistic documents. Together with his colleague Immanuel Wolff, Zunz initiated the study of the existing community and and the processes at work in it as a legitimate field for research. In the terminology of their time, their work was called "statistical." In present-day terms, they engaged in something very much like modern sociological-demographic studies.[8]

Like that of any other science, the program of the Science of Judaism was laid out in disciplinary compartments. Zunz delineated three aspects of Judaism as areas for research: (1) the dogmatic aspect, in which the relationship of God to man was defined; (2) the historical or symbolic aspect, which took in the nature of the covenant between God and Israel and the various institutions which witnessed the covenant and with which the acts of religious life were bound up; and (3) the ethical and the juridic-societal aspect.[9] These differing aspects of the essential nature of Judaism exist in a variety of forms, each possessing its own characteristics. We look upon the dogmatic side of Judaism from the point of view of the ideational content of Judaism, the historical side from the point of view of the development of the people and its institutions, and the sociological side from the point of view of the ethical idea which motivated social action.

The world of Judaism appears in all these aspects; it is composed of innumerable elements and forms a multiplicity of associations within and outside the boundaries of Judaism. Research resolves Judaism into its individual components, since its objective approach is analytical.

Zunz also marked off two general areas for critical research: doctrine or the ideas of Judaism, and grammar or language studies. Alongside these he placed the field of history, embracing language and ideas from the time of their origin until the present.[10] History does not disclose anything new in the content of Judaism; it does not deal with phenomena unknown to the other two areas but only adds a new perspective. The historical understanding of the development of ideas has been neglected up to now, declared Immanuel Wolff in his programmatic article, "On the Concept of the Science of Judaism," because the center of attention has been on the theological investigation of the content of ideas from the point of view of their religious-normative significance. The time has come to regard these phenomena in their true time context and to begin real historical research.

To the Science of Judaism history was really the starting point for understanding all phenomena. Every given datum, every law, document, idea or event was only the result of historical process. This process and the changes occurring in it were not, of course, apparent at any given instant. It was necessary to bring a longer duration of time into focus in order to discern the process and determine its content. Yet the technical difficulty involved in this did not invalidate the view that the process was constant and ongoing. Only a recognition of the historical nature of phenomena and their absorption in the process could lead to their understanding.[11] The Science of Judaism was therefore not satisfied merely to regard Judaism as a legacy of the past and as an object for historical investigation; it sought to understand the historical processes within Judaism which in fact had molded Judaism.

This historical process was first established (logically rather than chronologically) in respect to the relationship between the religious idea of Israel and its acceptance by the people, between the idea in the abstract and concretely in the life of the Jews. The Science of Judaism emphasized in its program that one of the distinguishing features of the historical development of Judaism was its attempt to arrive at a true recognition of the religious idea which corresponded to and coincided with its content. At first a barrier interposed itself between the religious idea as it had been defined in theoretical terms and as it existed in the concrete consciousness of the people. The development which occurred in Judaism was seen as a progressive improvement in the grasp of the religious idea. Religious consciousness rose from the sensual to a more elevated stage in which God was conceived of as personal and then to an even higher level where God appeared in the world as a whole. Thus the division of the Jews into the two kingdoms was connected with this process of progressive refinement. The Kingdom of Judah reached a higher level of religious consciousness than the secessionist tribes which formed the Kingdom of Israel.[12]

This view of the nature of the historical process in Judaism was a major departure in Jewish thought. The Jewish theological system, as it was formulated in the nineteenth century, recognized historical process and development as a fact, but only in the area of religious consciousness. It paid absolutely no attention to the historical process as it operated in the life of Jewish society as a whole and failed to see how the development of religious consciousness was intertwined with changes in society.

The philosopher Solomon Steinheim, a contemporary of the founders of the Science of Judaism, tried to show this connection in terms of the Jewish religion itself. He regarded the concept of a beginning in time as the distinguishing feature of any religion of revelation: Revelation, he said, is an act occurring in time and can be defined only against the background of time. After a pre-revelation period there occurs a break in time and then the revelation becomes a fact. Once the revelation takes place, however, its content does not change or develop in historic time. The content of revelation is a surprise gift, made once and once only. It does not enter into history. It remains forever separate from the historical process, since revelation, the appearance of the Divine, Who remains outside history, has no need of either time or history.[13] It is therefore possible to assert that there is no transition in time from one revelation to another. Any revelation is a breakthrough of new content, independent of history and unconnected with any previous revelation. Though each revelation occurs in time, the time process does not bind one revelation to another. Hence revelation as such has no history.[14] However, history enters the revelatory process in another sense, namely, through the subjective, human dimension. Mankind strives to grasp the objective content of revelation, and so continually advances. The active factor in this evolutionary process of revelation is man; it is we who develop through revelation and not *vice versa*.[15] From this point of view, history is external, having no contact with or influence on revelation. History and process are human facts related to the path of mankind striving to achieve a complete recognition of the religious idea which, in itself, is eternal and immutable. Progressing towards a full appreciation of the content of the revelation, mankind passes through the same stages of biological development as the idividual: from infancy to childhood, from childhood to adolescence and from adolescence to maturity.[16] One of the distinguishing marks of Judaism is the absence of any development in the content of its religious ideology, given in revelation. Process characterizes man, who is subject to change.[17]

This view of Jewish history as the realization of a religious idea which of itself remains fixed underwent serious modification as the Science of Judaism evolved. One such modification was Jost's recognition of the community as the unit operating in history.[18] In writing about the Oriental countries, Jost treated the Jewish community, which responded to its environment as a group, as a factor in Jewish history. Thus he added a social dimension to the concept of Jewish history by making plain the morphological differences between distinct communities of the Diaspora. Although Jost limited his study to the relations between Jews and the surrounding peoples and did not concern himself with processes at work in the Jewish community itself,[19] the basic importance of his contribution cannot be denied. It attenuated the view of Jewish history as tied to the religious idea by establishing a connection between the historical process and the actual life of the group.

Another modification of this view may be found in certain principles which Zunz evolved from his study of Jewish literature. Zunz distinguished between the Biblical and post-Biblical periods in Jewish literature, calling the first Hebraism, the latter Judaism.[20] In his opinion, the development of Judaism proceeded smoothly, undisturbed by sudden leaps.[21] This continuity attested to the connections between the various stages in Judaism, but without obscuring the differences between them. Development resulted from both internal and external causes, and only the combination of all the causes determined the character of each historic situation.[22] Changes in the historical process thus affected everyday religious beliefs and actions. Zunz saw as the turning point in the development of Judaism the work of Ezra the Scribe (5th century, B.C.E.), who ascribed a canonical character to Scripture.[23] In his overall view, history was thus a real process, not merely the path towards a fixed goal, to the attainment of a religious idea. Zunz implemented his theory only in one brach of Jewish literature, liturgy and ritual, but even if we agree in some respects with Hermann Cohen that Zunz was a mere collector of antiques, we must admit that in the underlying principles which he established he was a true historian. Jost's *History of Judaism*—the foremost work of its kind before Graetz—was doubtless an implementation of the plan formulated by Zunz for the study of the historical development of Jewish religious ideas.

To sum up: In mapping a program for historical research,

the Science of Judaism marked off two main lines of inquiry—
the study of the Jewish community in the concrete, and the
development of the religious idea. In effect, it laid the foundation
for the study of the history of the Jewish religion. The vision of
the scholars identified with this science, however, was in some
respects circumscribed. Their rationalistic bias restricted them
for the most part to the study of the rationalistic currents in
Judaism and Jewish history and excluded, deliberately or inad-
vertently, any other trends, first among which was the mystic.
Nevertheless, even in delineating the program of their activities,
they opened the way to the historical view of the evolution of
Jewish religion. By so doing, they took a stand between the
naive conception of Jewish history as progress towards the
attainment of an eternal ideal and the view which regarded the
ideal as interwoven with the process.

Judaism was presented in two forms: as an independent
entity and as a part of the general framework of history. The
Science of Judaism considered it an independent entity with
its own character, the proof of its independence being derived
from history itself, which established Judaism as a separate and
distinct phenomenon. History and historical research lead to the
inevitable conclusion that Judaism is separate and cannot be
absorbed into other topics of research. The historical fact of its
individuality and distinctness justifies and vindicates the special
study of the history of Judaism. In the early period of the Science
of Judaism, no one inquired about the factors which gave rise to
this independence and sustained it.[24] On the contrary, to the extent that the Science of Judaism was a consequence of detachment
from the living Jewish tradition, it was plausible not to ask what
sustained and preserved this Jewish separateness. Nevertheless, it
could have been asked what sustained and preserved Jewish individual existence *in days gone by*. To the extent that the Science of
Judaism inquired into the fundamentals of Jewish separateness, a
simple answer could have been offered: it was the religious idea
pervading Jewish life which kept it alive.[25]

However, the broader perspective of the Science of Judaism, and what distinguished it particularly, was something else again. Jewish individuality, as an area for research, was an established fact. But as a historical fact, interwoven with and an aspect of historical relations as a whole, it had yet to be explored. In arrogating this broader territory to itself, the Science of Judaism proceeded from the assumptions that the totality of spiritual life was reflected in Jewish activities, just as it was in activities outside the limits of Judaism,[26] and that Jewish literature was one of the aspects of this general expanse of spiritual activity.[27]

The study of any one such aspect did not involve losing sight of its relationship to the whole. On the contrary, the whole could be comprehended by recognizing the particular character of each part. It was the essence of historical research to proceed from details, from individual constituents, to the total organism they comprised, and the whole could not be grasped without an understanding of these parts. To comprehend the overall spiritual system was thus the main, true goal of historical research, the study of the particular and partial manifestations being, as it were, a means to this end. Judaism, though an independent historical fact, was bound up with the totality of spiritual manifestations.

This totality was given the rather indefinite name "spirit," or even "Divine spirit,"[28] phrases which had no precise denotation and functioned as catch-calls for all manner of cultural and historical activity. Perhaps the very vagueness of the terms was meant to imply that the real content of spirit lies in specific historical manifestations, of which Judaism is one. Since literature and language were thought to be keys to the understanding of this spirit, the Science of Judaism accordingly assigned great importance to the study of literature. This bias was acquired by the Science of Judaism from the Historical School, whose purpose was the discovery of spirit. However, the Science of Judaism was not drawn to this view by idealistic hopes only; it wished also to secure its own historical position. As we may recall, it proceeded from the assumption that Jewish literary creativity had reached a standstill and had even begun to decline.[29] If life is reflected in literature, then Jewish literary inertia, in this view, must be a sign of the inertia of Jewish life.

The study of literature in general was the heritage of the generation which gave rise to the Science of Judaism;[30] it was natural for the latter to view the study of Jewish literature as complementary to the study of literature as a whole. Yet there were differences among the exponents of the Science of Judaism as to what theoretical direction to take. Some argued that all literary works were expressions of a single content. Others maintained that each work was unique and differed from all others. But both sides agreed that all literary creations represented stages governed by the laws of evolution, and both embodied the general aspiration of arriving at a comprehensive view of literature as a whole.

The view that Jewish literature was a part of general human culture did not originate with the Science of Judaism. De Wette, one of Zunz's instructors at the University of Berlin, had recognized Jewish literature as a component of culture as a whole.[31] But such scholars and thinkers as de Wette and Herder had confined themselves to Bible studies, whereas the proponents of the Science of Judaism took post-Biblical literature as their main field of study. It was in recognition of the extent of this post-Biblical literature that Wolff asserted, in the article outlining his program, that the long attachment of millions of people to any uniform spiritual ideology of itself marks off an area for study. From the premise that historical-cultural activities express the spirit of the people, Zunz arrived at an outlook resembling Wilhelm von Humboldt's view of the nature of historical research. According to this view, no actual, specific situation could be understood except through an appreciation of the ideas which produced it. Ideas themselves were the creation of the reflective spirit, intuited, understood and seized by the genius, who recognizes them as they come into being. This intuitive power was characteristic of the artist, but also of the historian. For like the artist, the historian must encompass all details and work them into a single whole. He must see every part as relating to the whole. To evaluate the myriad scattered data, he must be familiar with the ideas which constitute the general background.[32]

Von Humboldt's shaping influence on the Science of Judaism was probably stronger that that of Hegelian philosophy, with which it is frequently associated, since Von Humboldt was less involved than Hegel in complicated metaphysical constructions. He was easier to follow, and his comprehensive view of history allowed the Science of Judaism to justify its existence.

As influential as Von Humboldt on this movement were the times themselves. It was the age of science—so the founders of the Science of Judaism believed. Yet while they sought to adapt Judaism to the spirit of the age, the adaptation was to be formal only. They had no intention of conforming to the prevailing climate of opinion in respect to changing social and political conditions. Their intent was to engage in a totally objective scientific investigation. For them, Judaism in accordance with the times meant a Judaism purified in the crucible of science, that is, Judaism studied and understood.[33]

Here the absence of romantic tendencies in the Science of Judaism is particularly noticeable. Its basic tenets were related to the age of rationalism rather than to the age of romanticism. Hence it could afford to disregard the anti-scientific and irrational trends current in its own time. In this respect, although the Science of Judaism arose in the 1820's, it was still tied to the 1790's in its evaluation of science and life in terms of intellect and reason. This evaluation led Eduard Gans, who witnessed the beginning of the Science of Judaism, to say that what his age wanted was to achieve self-consciousness—not only to exist but also to know.[34] Such attachment to the rationalistic, speculative temper, however, led to the difficulty shared with classic rationalism, that of accounting for religion in general and Jewish religion in particular. The Science of Judaism therefore seized upon the approach of German philosophy, which recognized religion as a value and sought to understand it as the crystallization of a rational idea.

THE DESIRE TO HARMONIZE with the spirit of the times also had a social and political dimension. The fathers of the Science of Judaism wanted access to the councils and salons of their time; as a division of scientific research, the Science of Judaism was to serve as their admission ticket. This entailed a somewhat precarious balancing act. For if, on the one hand, they were detached from the living, creative Judaism of tradition and used this detachment as the springboard for their historical researches, how could they, on the other, being Jews themselves, validate their claims to civil rights by their preoccupation with the very field from which they considered themselves removed?

The rationale for the Science of Judaism as a basis for Jewish rights is therefore somewhat strained, but we shall try to follow it nevertheless. Historic Judaism—the Judaism of the past from which all living attachment had been severed—was a spiritual manifestation, a structure from which many branches of creativity ramified, among them history, philosophy and poetry. These were equal in worth to the spiritual creations that had been wrought in areas outside Judaism.[35] Hence those who studied the works of Judaism and brought them to the light of all men were entitled to rights in the spiritual area and, by extension, to rights in society and the state. This claim was reinforced by the works emanating from the Science of Judaism themselves, by the spiritual maturity they expressed. Specifically, because these creative works were scientific and by definition the property of everyone, regardless of religion, they brought people closer together and put an end to the alienation of the Jew from his environment. The scientific study of Judaism did not differ from scientific study in other fields, regardless of its conclusions or discoveries, and the very fact of engagement in scientific research conferred the right to press demands.

Insofar as value content was concerned, the scholars of the
Science of Judaism conceded that their claims were not founded
on their own deeds but on the subject matter of the science itself.
Their position might be presented thus: we are studying a great
tradition; we are educated people doing research. A new basis
for civilization was being created by science, and the Jew who
participated in this grand and noble undertaking was no less
deserving than anyone else.[36] The Science of Judaism would
serve as a guide in the search for objectivity. It would reveal
the Jews in their reality and determine their ability to live
on the same level as other citizens.[37] It would contribute to the
making of the modern world.[38]

CHAPTER THREE

The Eternal People and Its History

TO JEWISH THEOLOGIANS of the preceding generation the questions raised by the Science of Judaism were irrelevant. Judaism was eternal and inaccessible to all of the changes of history. Nachman Krochmal, however, took a middle position. Unwilling to accept the idea that Judaism was not eternal, he could not deny the historicity of Judaism, which he called the problem of his generation.[1] His approach to the problem was a direct one: if he could isolate the aspects of Judaism which were but the products of historical development and therefore not permanent, he would discover whatever in it was lasting and immutable and so be able to defend Judaism against erosion.[2]

Krochmal was born in Brody, Galicia, in 1785. He married at the age of fourteen, as was the custom of the time, and went to live in the home of his father-in-law, a rich merchant named Habermann, in Zulkiev near Lemberg. Free to study, he read Hebrew philosophy, but also the German philosophers Kant, Fichte and Schelling, as well as Hegel, whose system particularly attracted him. Krochmal wrote one book, in which he set forth his ideas: *Guide for the Perplexed of the Time*, edited after his death by Zunz (who also gave it its title) and published in 1851.

Differing as he did with the Science of Judaism as regards the death of Judaism, Krochmal nevertheless turned to that Science for answers to some of his own basic questions. To acknowledge that certain values were relative implied, in his view, that they had arisen through the historical process. Thus history would serve as a dye, the way certain organisms are stained on a microscopic slide, to mark off those concepts and ideas which were completely explainable by it.

A practical and, if you wish, an apologetic motive animated his approach; yet he was impelled by a reasoned, intellectual motive as well. His work entailed showing that some Jewish values had arisen in time and were therefore not absolute, but it also sought to establish the absolute nature of Judaism and its differentiation from other spiritual and historical cultures. Krochmal's ultimate purpose was to prove that Judaism is eternal, that even though Judaism enters into history and undergoes change and transformation, it does not suffer the fate of mortal things. His historical view oscillates between two poles: Judaism as absolute and Judaism as immersed in the historical process. The problems inherent in Krochmal's historical perspective arise from this dualism and from his desire to establish some equilibrium between the two conceptions.

KROCHMAL begins with the Spiritual Absolute. The Absolute is eternally present, not a historical element. It is metaphysical in nature, the source of all spiritual elements. The relationship between the Spiritual Absolute and the individual spiritual elements existing in the world and its peoples does not occur within the framework of history. The Absolute exists as and in itself; its manifestation requires no time process. But for this very reason, the Absolute provides no basis for assuming the reality of history. So it is necessary to conclude that the two poles, the Absolute Spirit and the actual events of history, exist side by side without being dependent on one another.

The absence of any necessary relationship between these two poles is made clear by calling to mind that the Spiritual Absolute, which is the source of Judaism, is not only a metaphysical entity but is also identical with God. This identification, however, raises a problem: is it possible to assume that the Deity, that is, the absolute reality that exists apart from the world and history, has any need of the historical process? Certainly it may be asserted, from religious motives, that both the world and its history need God, that their very existence gives evidence of Him. But it is difficult to maintain that God needs history for His sake. To declare that there is a necessary relationship between God and history is tantamount to asserting that God is dependent on history. Hence establishing a relationship between the Absolute and the process of becoming poses, according to Krochmal, a difficulty which arises from regarding the Spirit Absolute as God. If we posit a mutual relationship between God and history, we imply a historical god, a developing god, a god that is not eternally present, whose reality is not absolute and distinct from the world. Conscious or unconscious reasons prevented Krochmal from accepting such a view.

This reality, as God, is not only independent of history and external to it; it also does not intervene in the course of history. Since God is the Absolute Spirit having no aspect of personal will, it is impossible to hold that He actively intervenes in history to set or to change its course. While Krochmal often uses terms taken from the realm of religion, which sees God as personal, his metaphysical conception makes it impossible for him to describe the Absolute in these religious terms. Not only is the historical process autonomous and independent, but its specific emergence, its course and its laws are not dependent on any absolute.

From a certain point of view, however, a relationship between Spirit and the historical process can be posited without changing the essential nature of either. Spirit, Krochmal said, achieves its full power only "through the medium of a long period of time and a large number of people." By this he was not referring to the metaphysical nature of the Spirit as such, but to our manner of conceiving it.[3] Our conception of the Spiritual Absolute occurs in the time process; that is, it does not attain its full clarity at the revelation but only in the course of historical development. Even the people of Israel at the foot of Mount Sinai did not, in the mass grasp the true meaning of Torah until the time of the return of the exiles from Babylon, after the passage of a thousand years. The Absolute itself, however, like the revelation as conceived by Steinheim, is clearly not dependent on time. In contrast to Hegelian doctrine, it does need to become recognized, but the process of history is not the progress of the spirit in knowing itself. Conception is a human activity; it does not transcend human boundaries, just as the Deity does not trespass them. To sum up: insofar as a relationship exists between history and the Absolute Spirit, this relationship is established by our cognition. It is not inherent in the Absolute Spirit as such, nor is it woven into history as a succession of concrete events.

But Krochmal nevertheless required of historical research that it should discern the character of a people and the influence upon it of the Absolute Spirit at any given time. This assumes that the element of metaphysical Spirit does exist in the historical process and that it can be revealed by historical research—a logical contradiction. Here Krochmal's theory of history reveals the basic dualism which gives rise in it to several problems. History is autonomous, a primary dimension to be taken for granted. But history—and with Krochmal history usually means Jewish history—is also the medium of the Spirit, the substance of the Absolute, which is the ultimate substance of all history. Thus history is a primary field in a real time-occurrence; it consists of change, a concatenation of events. However, since it is connected to a metaphysical Absolute, it is also some manifestation of the latter, which from the point of view of metaphysics needs neither revelation nor history. Krochmal accepted this dualism and tried to place history and Spirit side by side: history is the account of a metaphysical element even though it is also the account of actual events. Hegel, too, had granted the existence of a succession of independent events, but he regarded them as fulfilling the mission of reason, thus, in a sense, fusing history and metaphysics. But Krochmal made no effort to create such a fusion. He accepted his own dualism as if it raised no questions.

However, this weakness in Krochmal's thinking offered an advantage to historical research. Since history was not bound to metaphysics, it could become an autonomous discipline, with historical forces alone determining and moulding it. Krochmal himself did not draw this conclusion, since he was not aware of the methodological implications of his reasoning, but it may be inferred from his writings as a whole. [His view of the relationship between Spirit and history did not compel any prejudgment of the sequence or relationship of events in time.]

IT MAY BE ASKED: if history is an autonomous entity, then how and by what means does Jewish history become dependent on Spirit? The answer, which solves a specific historical problem, is that Jewish history is cyclical in character.

After a period of flowering, a period of decay sets in, and then the cycle begins over again. The cycle is not powered by the Spiritual Absolute but by social and psychological forces (the disintegration and disappearance of creativity) and the rhythm of organic life (aging and dissolution). The Absolute, however, guarantees that after a period of decline, a period of regeneration and growth will follow. But this guarantee is not due to any revivification of the Abolute Spirit, since by its very nature the Absolute neither dies nor revives nor intervenes in the course of history. Thus Krochmal's statement that "the Spiritual Absolute has to protect us and save us from the fate of all temporal existences" is not so much a contradiction as an affirmation of the cyclical character of Jewish history. Since the Absolute Spirit is all-encompassing and infinite, Jewish history too continues with ups and downs but without ending. One notices here in Krochmal the lack of a transition from metaphysics to history.

The metaphysical element has to perform the function of history; the infinite element has to preserve the perpetuity of the process, the continuous course of Jewish history. That is to say, even though the historical process is autonomous, it needs the metaphysical to assure its continuation. If not for the metaphysical element, Krochmal saw, he would have been unable to maintain that any period of reawakening and revival following upon a period of decay involved the same subject. Here, it seems, he was wrestling not only with the religious question of the eternity of the Jewish people and the special historical laws which set it apart from other peoples, but also with the internal problem of the continuity and identity of the historical process. Since he saw no proof of this continuity within the historical process itself, he was forced to posit a non-historical element connected with history, that is, the metaphysical element of the Absolute Spirit, which the eternal process in history parallels or reflects in time. This bridge across his dualism went one way only, leading from the historical to the Divine, but not back again, since the latter, as has been said, has no need of history at all.

But the metaphysical element only fulfills a specific function in Jewish history—that of preserving historical continuity; it does not affect the actual succession of concrete, historical events. In other words, the dependence of history on the metaphysical applies only to the framework and not to the occurrences within it. History remains essentially autonomous.

However, the special character of Jewish history and Krochmal's particular concern with it must be borne in mind. The focus of this concern was not the relationship of one event to another, or the transition from one to another, but the continuity of substance which connected the events. This continuity was not integral to the actual historical process, to the events and their governing laws, but underlay their ultimate meaning. Krochmal was no doubt influenced by the German idealist philosophy of history, which regarded events not from the point of view of their inner relationships but of the idea governing them; in addition, however, his religious outlook has to be considered.

Judaism conceived of history as a chain forged out of a substantive tradition and of tradition as the continuous development of an eternal body of truths. Krochmal was not able to free himself entirely from this view.

IT IS POSSIBLE, at first sight, to regard Krochmal's approach to the actual process of history as another example of the drawing of analogies from living organisms, so prevalent in his day.

Underlying this practice was the view that history is an inseparable part of the evolution in nature and does not exist outside the limits of the general scheme of events in the world. According to this view, history proceeds as a slow growth, an adaptation to circumstances, an absorption and overcoming of obstacles. It makes no sudden leaps; it brings out latent potentialities. The course of this development is set from within history itself; the development is propelled by inner forces. Though the historical process consists of growth from a root, there is a certain progress in it. The positive and constructive prevails over the negative and destructive. There is thus a kind of grace in this conception as applied to history, where the builders outnumber the wreckers. Then the whole process can be seen as one of increasing humane values and human worth, with every human activity directed towards these ends. Although in nature itself the growth and flowering of an organism is followed by its death, the historical analogists, especially Herder, tended to emphasize the positive over the negative.[4]

Krochmal, on the other hand, emphasized the negative, the processes of decay and disappearance. There is a first stage of historical evolution marked by development and progress, but in the second stage there is an exhaustion of strength followed by decline and ending in disappearance. Thus we can no longer maintain that there is continuous accretion of values. On the contrary, in the transition from first to second stage progress is brought to a stop.

But this is not the whole story, for like organic life, history is made up of both growth *and* decay. And decay itself is not necessarily a denial of progress. Certain characteristics may disappear from a particular society in history and yet remain preserved in the historical process as a whole.

The grain of this idea can be found in Krochmal, where he discusses peoples that decline and disappear but whose spiritual elements are taken over by other peoples. Yet it cannot be ascertained to what extent such a transference is true progress, or how successfully values are thereby preserved, or whether there is then a consciousness of improvement. To maintain that history as a whole is progressive, even while individual stages pass in and out of existence, requires a concept of history as a whole, of a continuity of particular historical links, and such a conception is lacking in Krochmal.

However, this lack is not an oversight. To Krochmal, continuity can be said to exist only where the creative forces are awakened to rebirth after their decay. Hence continuity applies to Jewish history *alone.* Only there, in Krochmal's judgment, has creativity shown a capacity for renewal after its decline and apparent disappearance.

THOUGH KROCHMAL DID NOT REGARD HISTORY as an ameliorative process, as a garden in which each year the blooms are larger and brighter, his idea of decay was tied somewhat to the notion of historical-social life as biological in character. From this perspective, history is only an aspect of all organic life. Though it is effectively severed from the force of spirit, history has no individuality of its own, neither does it have its own specific nature nor its own laws which differ qualitatively from those of other organisms. Biological and not historical forces control and shape man and his institutions.

But not entirely: the disintegration of a community or people, Krochmal believed, may also be brought about by the prosperity it has achieved. In admiring the beautiful and the splendid, the people's desire for pleasure becomes inflamed and higher ideas become subservient to the senses and their satisfaction. Wealth and possessions, pride and haughtiness wax and proliferate; increasingly, the few dominate the many. So the causes of decay lie not only outside of history, in organic nature, but in history itself. The decline of a nation is the consequence of its attainment of a certain peak of development, a certain level of power and accomplishment or of self-realization. Once satisfactions are to be had in abundance, there is no longer any need for effort. Creative drive slackens and decay sets in.

The completion of any cycle in decay does not in itself constitute progress. It entails no spiritual growth, nor can it be regarded as the fulfillment of a destiny, like the clearing of a stage on which another people with a historic mission will play its part. The very basis of such an idea — that the historical process *as a whole* possesses continuity — is lacking in Krochmal. Decay is a necessary fact, an inevitable consequence of specific causes, but it is not the instrument of a designing reason. In essence, even Jewish history is not the fulfillment of a mission or destiny. Krochmal conceded that Divine Wisdom had chosen the people of Israel "to teach the absolute faith of the Torah to mankind," but his conception of God included no basis for that choosing, since to him God was impersonal. Even though Jewish history, where decay is followed by revival, is different from the history of other peoples, neither development nor the addition of new values can be found. To be sure, one may discern a certain limited progress in Jewish history. Only with the return from the Babylonian exile did the religious conception revealed at Mount Sinai become the common possession of the masses in its full purity. From that period onward, however, no real progress took place. "And from then on the Torah remained engraved on the tablets of our hearts and has never departed from our generations since." Even the progress that occurred between the Sinaitic revelation and the return from Babylon brought no additions to the old values, and no introduction of any new values. The change lay in the refining and purifying of the people's religious consciousness. And after the period in which religious consciousness matured, history continued. So Jewish history is not bound up with the idea of progress or tied to the realization of some purpose. It is maintained by its substance, the Absolute Spirit, regardless of whether any additional development, or the revelation of new truths, or the striving towards some goal, occurs or not.

Krochmal's cyclical theory was not intended to apply to history in general, but only to that area of history in which Jewish history occurred. The distinguishing characteristic of Jewish history was its continuation beyond the period of decay. But this exception to the universal rule did not exempt Jewish history from the forces which operate in history generally. Even after a period of revival has begun, the organic laws still operate and disintegration sets in as it did in the previous cycle, just as in the histories of other peoples. In Jewish history, however, there is the germ of renewal.

The idea that history proceeds in cycles was not original with Krochmal, and even in Jewish literature there was to be found a cyclical theory, in some ways similar to his, in the mystical book *Sefer Ha-Temunah.** There the Torah is declared to be the spiritual essence of the world process. This essence goes beyond any specific explanation, any given literary or linguistic formu-

---

* But there is an important difference between the cyclical theories formulated in ancient philosophy (as well as by Nietzsche, for example, in modern philosophy) and Krochmal's hypothesis. In the former, the recurrence of cycles is based on a limitation or absence of spirit, which also accounts for their repetitiveness. In the latter, it is the abundance of spirit that leads to ever new cycles following the decline of the old.

In this connection, it is interesting to compare Krochmal with Vico, to whom he is sometimes said to be indebted, despite a scarcity of information concerning Vico in the German literature of Krochmal's time. Vico postulated not only a repetition in the structural form of each cycle—from barbarism to heroism to humanism—but he also assumed that internal concrete relationships were similar as well. Thus the differences between the patricians and plebeians in ancient Rome were repeated in the opposition between the nobles and serfs in the Middle Ages, etc. Though Krochmal found a likeness of structure in all cycles, he distinguished between framework and phenomena, so that the latter could be dealt with independently and on their own terms, without regard to phenomena in other cycles. Thus Krochmal represents a distinct and significant difference compared with Vico. S. Rawidowicz stressed in his studies Krochmal's relation to Vico.

lation. The Torah is unconditioned and its manifold aspects are discoverable in the cycles of the world (*shemitot*). They determine the nature and characteristics of every sphere.[5] Whether Krochmal knew of this work or not, the basis for his own cyclical theory is the same: the abundance of spirit which animates Jewish history causes it to continue. The spiritual content of other peoples and nations is limited, so their historical processes are limited in duration, while Jewish history, out of its fullness, carries on and renews itself.

However, there is a cardinal difference between Krochmal and the author of the *Sefer Ha-Temunah*. The latter regarded the cycles and their appearances as radical changes in the order of the world, as cosmic and religious cataclysms, destructions of values. Every new world cycle had its own individual laws and structure, and the differences in nature between the cycles precluded smooth transitions from one to another. Upheavals occurred in which new aspects of the Torah, hidden during previous cycles, made their appearance. Not so to Krochmal. To him the relationships between the cycles were sustained by the fact that they all occurred in the realm of history. The continuity is smooth, and the later cycle evinces no radical changes in the pattern of the world or the order of life found in the earlier.

Indeed, at just this point, a basic difficulty confronted Krochmal: how account for the transition from one cycle to another, the reawakening of creative forces within the cycle which had reached its terminus? Since the seed of a new flourishing cannot lie in disintegration, the reawakening cannot be generated in history. Krochmal's answer was that it was generated by the metaphysical element deriving from the Absolute Spirit. All events from growth to disintegration are propelled by forces present in history, but the beginning of growth, the starting of the cycle, is spiritually determined. A religious motif is here preserved in significant form—of a beginning conditioned by something outside of history, by a metaphysical element which is identical with God.

Krochmal recognized that all cycles were not the same, that

changes occurred between one cycle and another. The second cycle in Jewish history, which began with the return from Babylon, was not a mere copy of the social and historical forms of the first. There were, nevertheless, parallels within different cycles. The decrees following the destruction of the Temple and the decrees in Spain, the Sabbetai Zevi movement and the heretical sect bore significant resemblances. The similarities were not criteria for evaluating particular periods of history or for the study of their phenomena, but they were useful in tracing cyclical evolutions, since some of these characteristics appear in periods of growth, others in periods of decay. While cyclical factors thus imposed a degree of system upon the historical process, they did not impair the independence of the individual historical phenomena. These were to be judged in a dual light: as they fitted into the general pattern of history, and in terms of their particular nature and significance. The cyclical phenomenon, moreover, fulfilled a methodological function. Since the historical process itself was cyclical, the determination of the place of a specific fact in any cycle fixed its location in the process as a whole.

In laying out a program of historical research, Krochmal did not dwell on periods and their cyclical evolution, but rather on the specific data which composed them. This, in his view, was a fundamental principle. Individual phenomena should be studied in the richness of their variety. Individual differences must not be obscured for the sake of establishing uniform structures. In actual practice, Krochmal still confined himself to problems connected with the beliefs and opinions of the Jewish people; he found no place for social problems. But his principles obviously had a wider importance than his application of them.

CHAPTER FOUR

Judaism Considered by the Historical Method

KROCHMAL proceeded from the eternal to the historical. Heinrich Graetz studied the history of Judaism and the Jewish people for their own sake, in the belief that only in its history could Judaism be understood.

Graetz, whose *History of the Jews* in eleven volumes was to supersede all earlier works in its field, including Jost's, was born in the province of Posen, Germany, in 1817. As a young man, he was deeply impressed by Samson Raphael Hirsch's *Nineteen Letters of Ben Uziel* and the cause of Orthodox Judaism. He began his literary career shortly after he entered the University of Breslau, by writing articles opposing the Reform Movement. Thereafter he figured frequently in controversy. In 1879, three years after the completion of his history, which he had begun to publish in 1853, he was charged, on the basis of a strong anti-assimilation statement he had made in volume eleven, of being a foe of Christianity and the German people.

The accusation placed him under a cloud for almost the remainder of his life. When the Union of German Jewish Congregations created a commission for the study of Jewish history in Germany in 1885, the foremost historian of the Jews was not invited to join it. But the importance of the *History of the Jews* could not be gainsaid. It has been translated into English, Russian and Hebrew and, in part, Yiddish and French, and to this day remains a standard work.

Before he proceeded in the endeavor, Graetz attempted to lay out the position from which he would write the story of his people. Like Krochmal, he accepted the essential position of history, but with a difference. Krochmal, as we have seen, hypothesized an oscillation between two poles of Judaism—as a metaphysical-religious system on the one hand and as an agglomeration of historical facts on the other. Krochmal tried to bridge the gap between these poles, but their separation still remained. Graetz took a decisive step forward, declaring that whoever failed to see Judaism in its historic perspective, failed to understand it at all. Judaism as history and Judaism as religion coincide, he said, since Jewish history is a manifestation of the substance of Jewish religion. As Graetz was a historian, it is perhaps not surprising that he took this view. But if we look at the essay, "The Construction of Jewish History" (1846), in which he heralded his life work, we will find reasoning that led him to regard any concept of Judaism outside the perspective of history as meaningless.

AT THE UNIVERSITY OF BRESLAU, at which he matriculated in 1842, Graetz had been taught that any complex of human ideas could be understood not through introspection, but only by way of historical experience, by pondering deeply on the course of events lying outside the individual. Man's self-consciousness was not a subject therefore for psychology, but for history. This objectivization of human creativity was a consequence of Hegel's sweeping assumptions about the nature of history and its position in the development of the Spirit. Graetz's instructor in philosophy, Julius Braniss, had been a particular influence in this regard.[1]

Thus when Graetz examined the various philosophical attempts—by the Science of Judaism and philosophers of Judaism—to define Judaism and its basic principles, he was not overwhelmed by the disagreements he found. Each of his predecessors had studied Judaism from one point of view or another; each had based his idea of Judaism on a specific body of content in accordance with his own assumptions. Graetz appreciated the resultant lack of concordance. In his eyes, the many concepts of Judaism revealed its rich spiritual substance, and all were true when viewed as particular aspects of the essential Judaism. They were false only when, by attempting to invalidate others, they set themselves up as *the* basic concept.[2] Graetz saw his task as that of reconciling all of the partial, seemingly conflicting, definitions of Judaism as basic elements of a greater and more inclusive system.

This reconciliation, he affirmed, could not be effected by thought or introspection but only through history—by the "historicization" of all conceptual views. Moreover, none of these views was valid except insofar as it entered into the course of historical events, thereby becoming an active, historical force. To put this another way, each specific concept of Judaism, in that it was specific, was true insofar as it was relative, but to the extent that it was separated from its relativity it was false. However, the relative nature of each concept could not be determined in isolation, but only within the whole historic framework. Thus history's function in defining the substance of Judaism is crucial. How does the time-process become elevated to this level of history? We shall deal with this question later on. For the present, however, let us observe one important consequence of Graetz's approach to Judaism as history: it entailed the abandonment of any speculative attempt to construct a systematic, abstract view. For Graetz systematic doubt served as a positive basis for the justification of a historical perspective.

Graetz sought, in particular, to reconcile two principal views of Judaism by converting them into aspects of Jewish history.

One view was of Judaism as a legal, political and social system; the other was of Judaism as a religion with an ideological or philosophical basis. Graetz had been made aware of the contradiction between these two views by the development which Jewish reflective thinking had reached in his time, largely in the writings of Mendelssohn, Steinheim, Hirsch and Formstecher.[3] Graetz avoided the temptation of a middle ground, since to him taking such a position seemed only an easy compromise. Instead, he posited what he called a "magic bond" between the political and religious principles, the connection being an inner and unbreakable one. This bond, however, was not something given at the outset but only became manifest in the historical time-process. The two principles appear in succession and, by their alternation, determine the course of Jewish history. Judaism, as far as its substance is concerned, appears then as the combination of the political element with the religious in its precise sense.[4]

Graetz made no formal distinction between the two elements as abstract categories of ideas. The divergence between them comes about only through the working of history. That is to say, the connection between them occurs in the flux of time only, and Graetz separated these elements only in respect of time, not by conceptual distinction.

THIS FUNDAMENTAL ASPECT of Graetz's approach becomes especially clear if we call to mind that he did not try to explain and prove the existence of the "magic bond" by logical deduction. He did not seek to find a transition point where the political and religious were linked, or a bridge connecting one to the other. Instead, he saw the bond appearing as a matter of fact in history. History, by its very nature, reveals the existence of the bond in the succession of its events, not in the simultaneous existence of ideas and attitudes in juxtaposition. Thus, after the first period of Jewish history, which bore the stamp of state and law, came the second, which bore the stamp of dogma and religion. The connection between the political and the religious was therefore not logical but chronological. In this belief Graetz was supported by a basic assumption of the philosophy of history of his time: that the historical process is rational or reveals rationality. He believed that the primary idea of Judaism was the revelation of the two aspects of its history, first separately and singly and ultimately united and interpenetrated.[5]

From the historical relationship, the transition in time, Graetz derived a conceptual relationship, the transition of content. This relationship, which is not a matter of succession in history but one of reciprocity, involves the "magic bond" between two other, constant components: the Jewish "tribe" (*Stamm*) as body and the Torah as spirit.

Judaism thus is not a religion in the narrow sense, or the history of a church which represents the development of a doctrine and no more. It is the evolution of a people as well. It is, primarily, the history of a culture, the bearers of which are not certain outstanding individuals, but the people as a whole.[6] The political dimension of Judaism, moreover, does not appear in an abstract legal formulation, a code of laws, but in a community as a social aggregate—in human form as the Jewish people. In the present period of Exile, of course, the political element is absent, the place of the state being taken by the social element in its narrowest sense. Even in his youth, therefore, Graetz was speaking of the "magic bond" between the Torah, the people of Israel and the Land of Israel.[7]

The people exists either in conjunction with the state, characterized by laws and statutes, or in terms of its peoplehood, which it assumes when the bond between it and the state is severed. The religious dimension, on the other hand, is constituted in the Torah and its many offshoots. No longer restricted to the conception of God, this aspect of Judaism embraces literary and ideological works as they are revealed and developed in Jewish history.

In his *History of the Jews*, Graetz broadened the two principles, the political and the religious, on which he had based his understanding of the structure of Judaism, to include the national as a continuation of the political dimension, and culture and ideology as a continuation of the religious. He found each of these dimensions characteristic of certain specific periods, and yet he made them the distinguishing features of Jewish history as a whole. In other words, while these elements were partial and relative factors determining the horizontal structure of Judaism (its order in time), they also appeared in one form or other, in the vertical structure of Judaism, as elements present in all periods of Diaspora history. Therefore it was possible for Graetz to speak of the eternity of the Jewish stock and to discover Judaism in the multiplicity, if not the dualism, of its elements, by using history as a unifying instrument.

To the two components of Judaism, the law and the dogma, Graetz added a third, not intrinsically bound up with either but pointing to the future—the messianic belief.[8] It has been said of Judaism that it is not a religion of the present but of the future. Graetz accepts the future as a dynamic of Jewish survival. Without belief in a Messiah there would be no sense in the hope "on which the people, as it were, lives." Judaism is tied to history, an actual time-process, because history is directed towards the future.

The definition of Judaism, whether it be historical or conceptual, is bound up in Graetz with something else again: the relationship between Judaism and paganism. When it first appeared in history, Judaism manifested itself as a negation, a denial of paganism. In this respect Judaism was a type of protestantism. Two main features distinguish Judaism from paganism: 1. Judaism is based on the concept of *creatio ex nihilo*, while the basic tenet of paganism is that out of nothingness comes nothing, *ex nihilo nihil fit;* 2. paganism is based on the belief that nature is an all-encompassing, self-propelling force; God is only nature in its ideal state. Paganism therefore leads to a denial of the freedom of the ethical will, since man's deeds are determined by the natural forces. Judaism, however, posits a gulf between the natural and the Divine. In its view, nature, as contrasted with God, is non-existent and only the result of the exercise of divine will.

In these distinctions Graetz conformed to the Jewish philosophy of his contemporaries, Steinheim and Formstecher, explicitly acknowledging his indebtedness to the former, though not the latter. Steinheim made *creatio ex nihilo* a basic feature of his thinking, pursuing the idea through its various ramifications and characterizing creation as an act of free choice, rather than a necessary, natural development. Formstecher explored the contradiction between spirit and nature and appears to have been Graetz's main influence in the matter. Graetz's description of Judaism as the "Religion of the Spirit" (in the Introduction to the first volume of his *History*) is the precise title of a work by Formstecher published in 1841 (five years before Graetz's preliminary essay). It may also be appropriate here to note the reappearance of the contradiction between the religion of nature and the religion of history, in Moses Hess's *Rome and Jerusalem* published in 1862.

We may have already inferred that in his definition of Judaism, Graetz stood partially on historical and partially on conceptual ground. In outlining the differences between Judaism and paganism, Graetz showed that Judaism was not merely a historic opponent of paganism, had not arisen solely in opposition to and in conflict with paganism, but comprised an independent system of belief. His use of the negative term protestantism to designate Judaism was a dialectic rather than a historical one — one that entailed a substantive ideological polarity rather than a relationship between events in time. Yet he never lost sight of the historical dimension, defining Judaism, in its inner development, in terms of its legal-political and its dogmatic-religious components, as well as in terms of its location in the development of the religious idea in general, by the contradictions between creation and progress, freedom and necessity, spirit and nature.

Thus, though Graetz's conception of Judaism was tied to a

historical view of its values and principles, in respect both to the course of Jewish history and history in general, it also involved value judgments, either explicit or implicit, on the superiority of Judaism over paganism. Here Graetz the historian identified himself with his contemporaries, the philosophers of Judaism.

WE HAVE ALREADY INDICATED that Graetz was able to assign a function to the historical process in Judaism as a system of thought, since in his view the process was the reflection of an idea—it gave concrete evidence of what was latently potential in the idea. The process was the manifestation of the substance in time,[9] like the sowing and cultivation of a seed. Within the concatenation of events was a spiritual core, the extensions of which reached beyond mere history, making of Jewish history the realization of an idea. This core, moreover, existed prior to and was in essence detached from history.

THE SPIRITUAL AND IDEOLOGICAL CONTENT of Judaism served Graetz as the means for delineating the periods of Jewish history and as the distinguishing features of the three major periods into which he divided it.

In the first period, the political and social element predominated. The focus of effort is upon national and political consolidation and on raising the people to an acceptable level of spiritual life. In this period, which ends with the destruction of the First Temple, the historical process fluctuates between the natural course of national life and a striving to actualize the conception of God.

In the second period, the scales become weighted on the religious side. Social and political activities declined in importance, and religion became dominant. The period ends with the destruction of the Second Temple.

Even though the people then went into exile, its unity was

preserved. The third period is characterized by intellectual creativity: Judaism becomes science, knowledge, and seeks intellectual self-recognition. Removed from its land and engaging in introspection, the people becomes self-aware.

Graetz found the first two periods of Jewish history essentially different from the third. In the former a certain content manifested itself which had not appeared before. True, this content was latent in the idea of Judaism, but it had not manifested itself in history—and from the historical point of view, manifestation is all-important. Graetz defined these two periods in terms of their new content. He could not so define the third period, which revealed nothing new. It was a period of self-examination, of contemplation of the content manifested in the two previous periods, during which the religious creativity of Judaism proceeded without any reflection as an unsophisticated creativity. As against the unmediated nature of the earlier periods, the third appears as a mediated attempt to understand Judaism, to become self-conscious. It does not, however, represent a fusion of the two previous periods, the legal and political basis of Judaism being absent in exile.

What reason did Graetz put forward, it may be asked, for the transition from the unmediated unsophisticated periods to the mediated and self-conscious one? The transition from the first to the second period was brought about by the richness of the substance of Judaism, which sought to manifest itself outwardly in the historical process, but this was not true of the transition which followed. Graetz answered the question in terms of the historical experience of the people. In the period of exile, the Jews were excluded from participation in the activities of the world around them; they could find no external outlet for their productive energies. Hence the most outstanding among them created a world of inner thought.[10] This advance from the naive to the self-conscious stage, then, was not the fruit of an inner development, the outgrowth of an idea, but the consequence of circumstances which bore no relationship to the ideological

substance of Judaism. It is well to point out that in this circum-
stantial explanation Graetz was not unique. Furthermore, his
conception of the development of Jewish history is conditioned
by certain metaphysical assumptions, which are not explicitly
stated and which deserve to be examined.

Hegel regarded the dialectical progression as consisting of an
ascent from the unmediated to the mediated stage, as a chain
of concepts lying unexplained on a lower level and becoming
intelligible on a higher level, not by being newly given but by being
postulated and rationalized. The difference between the unmediated and mediated stages is therefore only relative, every
stage being unmediated as compared with the stage just above it.
Yet the very rhythm of the dialectical process depends on this
transition from the unreflective to the conscious. Graetz took
this formulation and transposed it from its conceptual context to
the area of history.

Graetz also borrowed from Hegel in another respect. Hegel
regarded religion as a lower stage than philosophy, as unmediated
in comparison with philosophy, which is composed of concepts.
The advance from the stage of religious imagery to that of
conceptual philosophy was, in addition, a development *within*
consciousness, ascending to ever higher degrees. This progression,
too, Graetz placed in the area of history. Religious creativity
itself, which manifests an ideological content, is by nature
unmediated. It is not self-conscious, does not reflect upon itself
in order to know itself. The study of religious creativity is
reflective; hence it is superior to its object. This reflection is not
only philosophical but also involves knowing and formulating
—it is science. Hence Judaism as a science is on a higher level
than Judaism as religious creativity. What was a stage in the
evolution of self-consciousness for Hegel became a stage in the
advance of the historical process for Graetz.

Here Graetz also reflects the aspirations of his time. As a
member of the generation engaged in the Science of Judaism,
he did not regard his scholarship and that of his contemporaries

as a mere isolated enterprise but as a link in the chain of Jewish history, as an epochal advance. As he saw it, Judaism was emerging from the state of an unreflective religion and acquiring a new outlook produced by reflective thinking—an outlook crystallized in the Science of Judaism. His expressed view was that the Science of Judaism added nothing to nor enriched Jewish creativity. It was a secondary phenomenon, beginning after Jewish creativity had exhausted itself. To this extent Graetz adopted the position of the Science of Judaism.

BUT REFLECTIVE THINKING, the distinctive feature of the third period of Judaism, also fulfilled a historic function: it acted as a preservative force. Self-conscious Judaism, by defining its nature in conceptual terms, is able to distinguish between itself and the phenomena it encounters in its historical process. This is the essence of Diaspora history. By not being part of any particular environment, the Jews become a universal people. By not merging with their surroundings, they maintain their integrity and independence. So viewed, the Talmud and its spirit are not a deviation from the path of Judaism but necessarily follow from the basic premise of Judaism as a protest against polytheism and pantheism and the religion of nature which both embody.

Greatz did not regard Judaism as a phenomenon of culture in general, nor did he try to find a connection between Judaism and general history. In the essay outlining his program, he cited the analogy between Judaism pursuing its individual path and a current in the ocean. However, far from signaling the end of Judaism, the Science of Judaism was an expression of its will to survive.

SO MUCH FOR the substance of the historical development of Judaism, according to Graetz. As for the formal structure of that development, the laws governing it, we learn little either from Graetz's preliminary essay or from his *History*. In the Introduction to the first volume of his major opus, Graetz announced that he wished to engage in the study of Jewish history, his mind free of theological preconceptions, concentrating on the general laws of history. Yet he remained silent as to what these laws were. He seems to have accepted the widely prevailing view of history as a process of sprouting, growth, maturity and decay (in Krochmal's words, emergence and growth, vigor and activity, decay and disappearance). But Jewish history is unique. Its development, in its area, begins over again; decay is followed by new growth and vigor. The cycle of rise and fall has in fact occurred three times. One cannot help being reminded of Krochmal here, although in actuality Graetz was probably not influenced by Krochmal's theory of cycles.

Krochmal's *Guide for the Perplexed of the Time* had been published in 1851 and was available to Graetz when he was working on the first volume of his *History* two decades later. And in the preliminary essay, written before Krochmal's *Guide*, there is no explicit reference to historical cycles. Yet the brief description of Jewish cyclical history appearing in the Introduction to Graetz's first volume differs substantially from Krochmal's systematic exposition, and shows no interest in the logical and historical problems with which Krochmal was prepared to deal.

The structural form of the historical process described in "The Construction of Jewish History" is different from the the notions of organic structure we find in the volumes of the *History* itself. However, the latter are consistent with the former with respect to the division of Jewish history into three "phases," as Graetz called them, tracing the transition from one phase to another in each period. Despite their essential differences, none of the periods is completely dissociated from its predecessor or successor; none is a closed circle. Yet Graetz never explained why Jewish history followed the particular course it had. We may infer as the reason the need of the ideological content of Judaism to manifest itself in history. After the political aspect of Judaism had been achieved, the religious aspect sought to be expressed, and so Jewish history passed from its political to its religious period. It might justifiably be asked why the political preceded the religious period chronologically, since from the ideological point of view both elements are components of the overall idea. Graetz offered no theoretical reason for this. He merely derived the sequence from his observation of concrete events. It may be, however, that his value judgments compelled it, the political stage being lower than the religious in the Hegelian progression.[11]

CHAPTER FIVE

Sociological Shift and Ideology

BY THE END OF THE NINETEENTH CENTURY the direction of Jewish thought had altered. The historical approach to Judaism had gained broad ground, while other points of view—and especially the religious-metaphysical one—had been called into doubt and put on the defensive. The work of Simon Dubnow, who began in the 1880's as a follower of Graetz, was in the new historical tradition, but it entailed a significant shift from ideas formulated as determining Jewish life to the Jewish people as a social entity.

The development of Jewish historical writing in this period generally is characterized by a gradual transfer of interest from the description of events to the searching out of the laws inherent in their flow.[1] This cannot be accounted for entirely by the emergence of a more penetrating discipline. Nor can it be imputed wholly to a sense of obligation to Jewish historiography felt by later historians to complete the work, already begun, in tracing formative and operative causes in the flow of historical events. There is another, more fundamental reason for the shift, one the historians themselves were not always conscious of: the fact that the historical approach was no longer seriously challenged and the misgivings it once had evoked were now of small effect. The need for indirect endorsements by appeal to uncontroversial premises had passed, and it became possible to examine the ways that history worked without distraction. From a beginning in which it had to feel its way through the realm of eternal values, Jewish historical thought had evolved and matured to the point where it could deal with spiritual matters in a historical light and in accordance with definite ideas of what comprised history.

Dubnow's work affords the clearest evidence of this evolution. Born in 1860 in the province of Mogilev, Russia, and living on into World War II (he was killed by the Nazis in 1941), Dubnow attempted to create a synthetic, synoptic account of Jewish history, basing his endeavor on the assumption that the Jewish people is "the most historical of all peoples."

What he meant by "historical" is not unambiguous, and Dubnow defined the word in at least two different ways. A people is historical if it has created cultural values that have left an indelible mark upon humanity. (On the other hand, a people is non-historical if it has left no such notable trace.) In this sense, a people's historicity is an index of its creative power. The people which produced the Bible and instituted monotheism is thus a historical people. But a people is also historical in terms of its duration as an entity in time. Some peoples are more historical, in this sense, than others. The span of the Jewish people's existence leaves no doubt as to its historical status, duration-wise.

But there is a qualitative difference between these definitions. Whereas a study of the traces left by a people and its literary and historical creations draws a line of demarcation between the two classes of peoples (historical and non-historical), a survey of historical peoples' life-spans in time establishes distinctions within the class itself. Chronological limits are not a criterion for determining the place a people occupies in world history, nor are they a measure of the influence wielded by that people upon the course of human evolution. Its life-span is but an attribute of a people considered in itself, within the limited confines of its affairs, and has no bearing on history at large.[2]

Dubnow's point of view is reflected in his idea of nationality, which we shall presently discuss in detail. In this context it will suffice to touch upon those of its aspects which are related to the underlying principles of Dubnow's historical thought. The character and status of the Jewish people of his time were, according to Dubnow, the work or result of history. A people's life unfolds within the time-process. At its inception that life is of an ethnical-natural character. The next stage of its growth is the political-territorial one. Finally, the people outgrows its territorial need and rises to the cultural-historical level of existence. The Jewish people, having passed in and through all these stages, had attained the highest level of national existence — the final, crowning phase of peoplehood. And this had occurred only in history. For outside of history a people can neither exist nor be understood.

The crucial importance of history on the character of national existence can be seen from another angle. The basis of a people's life lies in the subjective ties that bind its members to its history. The individuals are aware of their connections to the group only insofar as they consider themselves bound to its history. History engenders the people, and history consolidates it into an integral whole. In other words, the historical process as a given fact is the assumption from which any study of the evolution and national destiny of the Jewish people necessarily proceeds; and this is the point of departure of Dubnow's work.[3]

Unlike Edmund Burke in English thought or Ahad Ha-am in Jewish thought, Dubnow does not make a point of the historical heritage passed on from generation to generation, but rather emphasizes the historical process itself and the changes that it brings about. It was the character of his historical conception, together with his commanding view of the broader historical vistas, that led him to reject the idea of an eternal people existing outside of time or indefinitely in it.

We have seen that Krochmal had tried to establish the

eternity of the Jewish people and to present it as the reflection of the people's absolute spiritual essence. Krochmal employed the concept of eternity in his historical theory after carrying it over from the metaphysical-religious to the historical-temporal realm. Dubnow, for whom the historical approach was unchallengeable from the very outset, in contrast rejected such metaphysical notions as "eternity" or "the Absolute."[4] History pertains to a duration of events that lends itself to measurement and determination in terms of the particular time of the events' occurrence. Eternity is by definition timeless. An enduring people is not necessarily an eternal people; it is a people living in history from antiquity up to the present. The Jewish people's historicity, the span of its life in time, has invested it with its singular quality of an "undying" people, but its life in time is nevertheless finite and can be gauged.

In the light of Dubnow's theory, the idea of an eternal people lacks all of its primary content. A historical approach excludes the possibility of employing religious or metaphysical concepts which remove their objects from the domain of history. According to Dubnow, the events constituting the life of the Jewish people are historical *par excellence*. The singularity of the Jews' status in history is not due to its detachment from the process, but precisely to its being rooted and persisting in it.

DUBNOW'S SOCIOLOGICAL PERSPECTIVE, the most familiar aspect of his historiography, affords further evidence of the governing principle of his work. The sociological approach to historiography implies that the subject matter of historical research is the people, that is, "the national personality, its genesis, growth and struggle for survival."[5] Historical research so slanted is not concerned with literary and spiritual values; it treats the various values as expressions of the people's character. Since spiritual values are the offspring of the people and cannot be taken as independent of it, historical research should deal with values not in terms of their material, religious or literary significance, but in terms of a people which cannot be understood save as a living community. Thus the sociological perspective represents a further step away from the realm of eternal values toward concentration on the temporal domain. The primary assumption that the latter alone constitutes the ground of historical reality justifies the idea that history can be understood in its reality only from a sociological point of view.

The actuality of the temporal process is a motif that runs through all of Dubnow's thought. To understand the character and situation of a people one must study its historical development; to understand national history one must look upon the people as a community living in time. History is both the starting point and the terminus of any investigation of a people. In this sense, Dubnow may be said to have completed the circuit of the historical approach to Judaism. He proceeds on the assumption of the people's historicity and arrives at the conclusion that the people's history is its only reality. The first step is from history to the people; the second is from the people back to its history.

The sociological phase of Dubnow's thought may be regarded as an attempt to work out ideas put forward by the fathers of Jewish historical thought. Or it can be taken as a supplementary perspective extending the field of historical conception beyond the spiritual-creative formulations stressed by Jost, Graetz and Krochmal. It can also be considered as a reflection of the social agitation of the times and a result of attempts to found a Jewish movement which would be social and contemporary in its basis and historical in its content. That all these factors are operative in Dubnow will emerge from a consideration of his programmatic conception of Jewish national existence.

But before turning to this, we must make a critical observation. The historical and sociological approaches to history are not identical, nor is there any intrinsic reason why they should be. The historical viewpoint reduces the history of a people to its development in time; the sociological assigns primary importance to the social factor in the historical process. One may deny the applicability of the concept of eternity to a people as a social unit, as if any people occupies a singular position in the course of historical events. But it is by no means clear whether the concept of a people can be divorced from the factors which form and mould its way of life—its literature or the practices and beliefs which define its spiritual values and aspirations. One need only recall the part played by the *Halakhah* in the shaping of the Jewish people's pattern of living to see that this is so.

Thus the sociological approach to history is a supplementary perspective induced by considerations which do not necessarily follow from the historical approach itself. Yet it is quite true that without the latter, with its rejection of metaphysical and religious concepts, there would be no logical or philosophical grounds for taking a sociological position, either.

Dubnow's conception of the sociological component in history is somewhat unclear. He was inclined to distinguish between the foundation of national life, which to his mind comprised its organizational and institutional elements, and its superstructure, or the totality of its creative works. He apparently believed that society constituted a living entity without regard to this superstructure. But a society is not an organism in the biological sense, nor is it independent or entirely distinguishable from its creation.

Were its concrete being not reflected in this superstructure, a people would not exist at the organizational or biological level, either. Take the struggle of the Jewish people as a historical community for its rights and status in the modern world. The character of this struggle is not analogous to an organism's search for nourishment in a hostile ecological environment. It presupposes a definite attitude towards history and the Jewish people's place in it. Thus, for example, a decision must be taken as to whether history constitutes an external framework that does not affect the way of life of a society or whether an anchorage in history is the *sine qua non* of national existence in its strictest sense. A social entity is non-existent without an awareness of the nature of society, in the light of which it contemplates and evaluates itself. What is and what is not sociological in the existence of a historical community, the character of which is defined by history—and Dubnow rightly underlined the relation between a people and its history—is not nearly as clear-cut, simple and unambiguous as would appear from the tacit or explicit presuppositions of Dubnow's theory.

IN ORDER TO ESTABLISH THE CONTEXT of Dubnow's views on problems of Jewish existence and their relation to his historical thought, it is appropriate here to touch upon the question of the Jewish people's extra-territorial existence. There are several attitudes towards extra-territoriality dictated by divergent concepts of what a people's existence is. In the strict sense of the term, "extra-territoriality" is a geographical concept denoting the existence of a people without specific geographical confines. But the term also has political and social connotations. The idea of the Diaspora as being extra-territorial is, in fact, the line of demarcation between the Zionist and non-Zionist, or anti-Zionist, theories of Jewish collective existence. For to see the predicament of the Diaspora solely in its extra-territorial character is also to imply that the problem of the Diaspora can only be solved by the abolition of extra-territoriality, that is, by a territorial ingathering of the people. On the other hand, if one holds the territoriality of national existence to be a primitive stage of national growth to be outgrown, one no longer conceives of the problem of Jewish national existence in geographical-territorial terms, or else one looks at extra-territoriality as a problem or anomaly to be overcome.

Dubnow held that national existence evolved from the material to the spiritual and from external simplicity to inner complexity.[6] Only at the so-called material stage of national growth is there a connection between the people and existing external factors, one of which is territory. At the stage when a people rises from the ethnic-natural level to the territorial-political level of existence, its life is framed by a political structural shell. This latter level, characterized by the ownership of or sovereignty over territory, is not based on bonds which are intrinsic and autonomous but directly on the fact of statehood. The transition to the next and final stage in the evolution of a people entails the disappearance of external criteria and their replacement by subjective ideals.[7] Now the people exists by virtue of its inner attributes.

From this point of view, the extra-territorial existence of the Jewish people is not an anomalous or undesirable political phenomenon but rather the highest attainable mode of collective existence, a level at which other peoples have yet to arrive. Jewish nationality, according to Dubnow, thus represented the quintessence of cultural-historical or spiritual peoplehood.[8] The extra-territoriality of the Jewish people, both in terms of its removal from a particular land and its life in dispersion, therefore bears witness to its exalted position among all peoples and also to its durability.

It is true that one does come across passages in Dubnow which refer to the Diaspora as an external necessity that must be accepted, rather than as a desirable good or ideal. We resign ourselves, Dubnow says, to the historical necessity of the Diaspora and strive to preserve and cultivate the national existence of the greater part of the Jewish people which inhabits it.[9] Here extra-territoriality does not bespeak a high stage of national development so much as an inexorable fact. The Jewish people must take this fact into account, acknowledge its irresistible force, and endeavor to fortify national existence within the limits it defines.

In the last analysis, however, Dubnow's position with regard to the Diaspora remains constant. For both his theoretical premise and his practical assessment lead to the same conclusion: the extra-territorial Jewish people must build its life within the given framework of its dispersed existence. According to his premise, there is no need to provide a territorial basis for national existence; practically, there is no possibility of providing such a basis. And in either case the problem of the Diaspora is the same: to find a way of safeguarding the people's spiritual-creative powers or, at the very least, of preserving its cultural independence as a spiritual-historical entity. In laying claim to cultural autonomy, Jews must put forward historical demands so that they may be enabled to live not only as other human beings but also as sons and daughters of a particular historical people.[10] The solution to the problem of Exile lies not in overcoming it but in securing an organized way of life within the conditions it imposes.

Dubnow's practical program for safeguarding Jewish national existence is consonant with his theory of shifting centers of Jewish history. Over the ages, according to this theory, not one but several territorial centers have served as the focal points of Jewish national life. Thus even the social and cultural creativity of the Jews as manifested in their history is independent of geography. To put this another way, extra-territoriality—in the basic sense of dispersion and detachment from a single center—is the distinguishing mark of the Jewish people not only in space but also in time—from the land of Israel, then via Babylon and Spain to the shifts in Jewish existence in the nineteenth and twentieth centuries.

Jewish activity should therefore aim at fortifying the existing national center, which in Dubnow's time was essentially the Jewish community in Eastern Europe; it must strive to keep abreast of and serve the evolutionary development of Jewish history at every stage. In the course of time the center of gravity of Jewish life might shift to an area other than Eastern Europe, but this would make no essential difference. The spiritual nature of Jewish existence would remain unshaken, no matter what external circumstances prevailed. Thus the program for Jewish activity in the Diaspora and for the Diaspora's sake springs organically from the idea that collective existence apart from territory is not a problem which calls for change in the pattern of Jewish national existence.

We have seen how Dubnow's approach to national problems dovetails with his historical theory, according to which national character and status are both products of history. It is impossible to alter either. Since the people's extra-territoriality is bound up with its history, to try to change the situation would be both futile and undesirable. For one thing, it would result in a regression from the present spiritual stage to a previous one, less advanced. For another, as Jewish history has been enriched by migration and the transplantation of national centers, so it would be impoverished by being confined to one population and one place.

It would appear that Dubnow did not believe in the possibility of a national renaissance in the sense of a return to national roots. Indeed, he recommends moving with the historical trend as it emerges. But the matter is not quite this simple. Though he seems to be saying that we must accept the direction of history, he does not believe that this direction can be followed as a matter of course. Rather, he saw the need to translate it into a specific plan of action. This plan of action did not embrace a comprehensive way of life but embodied a struggle for political and cultural rights in the countries where Jews lived. Dubnow was inclined to propose such a plan for the Jewish community in the United States with revisions dictated by the different conditions there. It may be that the programs proposed by others for enriching Jewish life in America, by way of organized, comprehensive institutions, reflected Dubnow's ideas, at least as far as some of their sponsors were concerned. For Dubnow's plan was in no way related to territory. Even the establishment of a Jewish community in Palestine could not alter the course of Jewish history. The Palestinian community would be a further example of the pattern of Jewish history, another link to the chain of national centers in time past, another locus in the network of centers in the present.

THERE IS, however, a certain tension between the historical and sociological aspects of Dubnow's thought. The prominence of the sociological motif and method in his thought underlines the organizational and institutional aspects of national existence. Now, evidently, territorial and political elements are among the constitutive factors of the institutional phase of national life emphasized by the sociological approach; but from a historical viewpoint their necessity is open to question—unless they are taken to be lapses from the already achieved extra-territoriality in earlier stages of Jewish life. In the end, Dubnow had to find a non-territorial substitute for territoriality, and his way out of the dilemma was by way of Jewish political autonomy and communal cultural rights.

For territorial consolidation Dubnow substituted political-cultural consolidation—the organized cementation of Jewish existence by legal means and administrative bodies with a network of schools and research institutes. Thus, ultimately, Dubnow does not accept the absolute rationality of extra-territoriality, but rather tries, within the framework of extra-territorial existence, to find the advantages afforded by territoriality.

This being so, one cannot help wondering whether autonomous existence in the Diaspora within an extra-territorial context is indeed historically superior to territorial existence, which grants a certain measure of autonomy as a matter of course—autonomy not despite the lack of territory but precisely by virtue of territorial sovereignty, autonomy within the framework of, and guaranteed by, a Jewish rather than a non-Jewish state. The issue at stake is not the technical one of whether and to what extent extra-territorial autonomy could, practically, be achieved, but why Dubnow did not go the whole way toward territoriality and admit that it is operative in its original basic sense. For all his emphasis on the sociological aspect of Jewish history and existence, Dubnow finally turns out to be a spiritualist, like the fathers of modern Jewish thought against whom —implicitly or explicitly—he set himself.

Be this as it may, it is clear that the diverse aspects of Dubnow's thought—the strictly historical perspective *qua* historiographical theory and the national perspective *qua* ideology—are interrelated. This is not to suggest that in his historical theory Dubnow is the mouthpiece of ideological thought. Nor can it be said, without reservation, that Dubnow's ideology is the practical translation of his historiography. At the same time, however, as has been stressed, there is certainly a connection between these two distinct facets of his thought, a connection enhancing the image of the historian and national thinker which casts a reflection on both the historiographical and national facets of his work.

With the shift from values to peoplehood, the nineteenth-century idealistic scientific momentum came to an end. Yet the questions Jewish thought raised in that century would re-emerge in our own against the background of the Jewish renaissance, to whose problematic situation—and its expressions—we shall now turn.

PART THREE

Peoplehood
and Its Past

CHAPTER SIX

National Revival
and Traditional Values

THE RISE of historical consciousness in Jewish thought brought about a weakening of the bonds of tradition, which could itself be subsumed under history and therefore could no longer be regarded as a super-historical norm. The beginning of a movement for national survival produced a counter-trend: an examination of Jewish values *versus* and within Jewish history. One of the chief figures in this development was Ahad Ha-am.

Ahad Ha-am (the pen-name means "one of the people") was born Asher Ginzberg in 1856 in the province of Kiev, Russia. The son of a prominent Hasid, he received a thorough Jewish education and married at sixteen. Later he traveled to Western Europe and studied at the universities of Vienna, Berlin and Breslau. Returning to Russia, he was drawn to the movement called Hibbath Zion (Love of Zion), led by Dr. Leo Pinsker in Odessa, not so much as follower as sympathetic critic.

The basic features of Ahad Ha-am's thought can be discerned in the three main controversies in which he was now to become involved. The first concerned questions relating to the management of agricultural settlements in Palestine by Hibbath Zion during the last two decades of the nineteenth century. The

Hibbath Zion movement was founded in the 1880's, mainly by Russian and East European Jews, for the purpose of establishing such settlements and improving their conditions. When the settlements began to falter, Ahad Ha-am charged Hibbath Zion with failure to screen prospective applicants for *aliyah* settlement as to their personality and moral character. The inadequately trained immigrants, he said, lacked "preparation of the heart"—a phrase which later became a social and ideological watchword. In Ahad Ha-am's view, the crisis in which the movement found itself was essentially psychological and ethical, and out of the resultant controversy there emerged one of Ahad Ha-am's central concepts, namely, that settlement in Palestine was first and foremost the concern of an elite which had to be prepared for its task spiritually, ethically and ideologically. The conditioning of this select group was an indispensable prerequisite to successful settlement in Palestine.

The second controversy centered upon the basic principles of political Zionism in the early days of that movement. In this dispute one must be careful to distinguish the practical from the theoretical aspects. With regard to the former, Ahad Ha-am shared the view of the successors to Hibbath Zion who argued that Theodor Herzl's political Zionism neglected practical work and achievement in its Palestine program and relied solely on external political conditions to advance the work of settlement. They further pointed out that political Zionism was not favorably inclined towards cultural activities and that it failed to recognize that a renewal of the Jewish spirit was indispensable to Jewish revival generally. Steeped as he was in Jewish tradition, Ahad Ha-am also chided the founders of political Zionism for their ignorance of Jewish culture, as reflected in their private views and public programs. The theoretical phase of this dispute focused upon a basic disagreement as to the central objective of Zionism. We must consider this difference in detail after describing the third controversy in which Ahad Ha-am took part.

This last controversy was in the province of literature and concerned the nature and aims of the new Hebrew expression. Ahad Ha-am advocated a more intense preoccupation with Jewish subjects and with the cultural resources of the Jewish past, so that the modern Jew would be imbued with a sense of the historical continuity of Jewish culture. This controversy and the second—though they fall within different areas—have a number of common features.

In one sense, modern Zionism has its origin in the preoccupation of Jewish thinkers with a satisfactory solution of the place of the Jewish people in the world at large. The attempts to resolve this problem gave rise to two schools of thought, one represented by Pinsker and Herzl, the other by Ahad Ha-am. The former analyzed the existence of the Jewish people from the vantage point of its relationship to the political and social environment in which it happened to find itself. The Jews were seen as rejected, the ideological and practical form of their rejection being anti-Semitism. To Pinsker and Herzl anti-Semitism constituted the fundamental problem of the Jewish people— what was then technically known as the Jewish Question. This point of view reflected the disappointment of Jews in the Emancipation which had seemed to promise them equal social and political rights. It is perhaps no accident that both Pinsker and Herzl were at first ardent advocates of Emancipation, and that they embraced—and indeed created—political Zionism only after the wave of disillusionment which followed the pogroms in Southern Russia and the Dreyfus Affair in France. We can appreciate the feelings that led to this change—the desire of Jews to become a recognized and accepted part of their society, and then their frustration on being spurned. Eager to join in the life of the people around them, they were driven instead into increasing isolation, so that the Palestine solution presented itself to them with particular force.

Ahad Ha-am's position was based on an altogether different assumption. The problem of the Jewish people, he believed, was that it was drawing too close to its environment, despite an admitted tension between the Jews and their surroundings. In fact, the more isolated they felt, the more intensely would the Jews be likely to feel a need to identify with the dominant non-Jewish culture by absorbing the latter's qualities, thereby attenuating their own uniquely Jewish qualities. The assimilative process Ahad Ha-am saw in the making in his own time had two precedents in Jewish history—Alexandrian Jewry in the last century before the common era, and Spanish Jewry during the Middle Ages.

This adaptation of Jews to an alien environment, he felt, would not only tend to vitiate the creative elements in Jewish culture, but would also jeopardize the inner unity of the people. Since the environments in which the Jews lived were politically and nationally far from uniform, the adaptation eventually would be to different cultures and traditions. Consequently, the Jewish people would break up into separate sub-groups according to the respective cultures its members sought to adopt. The chief task of Jewish revival was to check this disintegration and, by creating a new common basis, preserve the unity of Jewry amid the historical conditions in which it now was placed. In sharp contrast to Pinsker and Herzl, Ahad Ha-am held that the objective facts tended to draw the Jews and Judaism closer to, rather than further away from, their alien environment. Only the socio-national will, he believed, could have a restraining effect upon this tendency, by means of independent Jewish organization and the Palestine solution. Thus where Pinsker and Herzl posited the will, Ahad Ha-am posited necessity; and where they posited necessity, he posited the will.

The problem of the unity of the Jewish people as seen by Ahad Ha-am deserves to be examined more closely. Ahad Ha-am interpreted this problem from the standpoint of Jewish history in the Diaspora, seeing that the unity is basically a religious one. With the loss of the Jews' political and territorial center, the Jewish religion both as a faith and as an institution became the sole unifying force—a force which Ahad Ha-am viewed on the level of a historic factor. The Jews owed their oneness to a common past going back to the Bible, and not to any geographical area that they happened to occupy in common.

But the historico-religious bond that held the people together weakened progressively and threatened finally to disappear. Thus the fate of the Jews would be determined henceforth by their geographical dispersion, which dictated the conditions of their existence in all spheres, including their cultural life.

The primary task of Zionism, therefore, was to find a new unifying ground for Jewish national existence in the form of a Jewish center in Palestine, universally acknowledged by all Jews. The establishment of such a center would put a halt to the process of disintegration and would perform the function hitherto served by the Jewish religion and Jewish historical continuity.

The question to which Ahad Ha-am addressed himself he called "The Question of Judaism and Jewry" to distinguish it from the question which Pinsker and Herzl had posed and named "The Question of the Jews." The difference involved the national fate of the Jewish people as a historical and cultural entity, in contrast with their status in the society in which they lived or with their entitlement to equal social and political rights.

An additional distinction made by Ahad Ha-am had to do with the subject of Jewish revival. For whose benefit was this revival? Pinsker and Herzl were concerned with the individual Jew in his daily struggles and frustrations in an alien society, whereas Ahad Ha-am had in view all of Jewry as a whole. He furthermore expected that each individual Jew would place national existence above his private interests and personal status. Thus he connected revival with the task of an elite, though not in the technical, but educational sense he had in mind when criticizing Hibbath Zion. Rather, he demanded of this elite that it take upon itself extraordinary duties without receiving special privileges in return and that its members regard their personal fates as identical with that of the entire people and its historical destiny.

There still remained, according to Ahad Ha-am, a practical difficulty in connection with Jewish immigration to Palestine. For if one assumed the basic question to be that formulated by Pinsker and Herzl, it was obvious that its answer should not be framed in terms of the entire Jewish population of the Diaspora. Since the goal of political Zionism was, therefore, simply not feasible, Ahad Ha-am's solution was to create a "spiritual center" in Palestine.

THE IDEA OF THIS "SPIRITUAL CENTER" was expressed by Ahad Ha-am variously at different stages of his literary and public career. We are often led to believe that the concept arose as an alternative to Herzl's *Judenstaat*. However, Ahad Ha-am's mature, not polemical, view reveals no such opposition and no desire on his part to set up an antithesis to Herzl's political formulation, but rather something supplementary to that formulation and expressing a particular quality inherent in it.

Ahad Ha-am conceived the function of the center in Palestine to be "spiritual" by reason of the physical distance that separated the Jewish community there from other Jewish communities in the Diaspora. In terms of world Jewry, the influence wielded by Eretz Israel could only be "spiritual." But this was no small thing. The Jewish community in Eretz Israel would awaken among Jews throughout the rest of the world a desire to identify themselves with the Jewish people and its historic legacy. Occupying a specific geographic area in the present, this community would serve as a unifying force more powerful and effective than common experiences of the distant past. Ahad Ha-am's basic psychological and sociological assumption in this matter was that the Jews of the world would be eager to defer to the small Jewish community in the Holy Land. He understood, however, that the influence of Palestine Jewry would depend on the quality of life it achieved as well as on its spiritual and literary creativity.

IN REGARD TO THIS CREATIVITY, Ahad Ha-am believed that
the Palestinian community could become a spiritual center only
insofar as it was able to develop a conscious continuity between
the old and the new bases and that the spiritual elements of the
Eretz Israel community must be rooted in historic Judaism and
its spiritual heritage. Here, however, he was confronted with a
difficulty that lies at the very heart of his conception. The religious
basis of Jewish unity in times past — so he believed — had crum-
bled, and in the modern world religion no longer performed its
traditional functions. The question as to whether Jewish historical
continuity was to be explicitly religious in character was answered
by Ahad Ha-am in the negative. The new Judaism would respect
the Jewish religion as a significant creation of the people, but the
Jewish revival would not be necessarily subject to its imperatives,
or at least be free to reinterpret them.

Two reasons, one historical and the other theoretical, accounted for this view. Historically, it could not be expected that
the generation to which Ahad Ha-am addressed himself would
forsake its contemporary attitudes on account of a continuity
that no longer was. Theoretically Judaism, as Ahad Ha-am
understood it, was not essentially a faith but a system of ethics.
Ahad Ha-am was, no doubt, deeply influenced by the positivistic
currents of thought prevalent in the nineteenth and in the early
twentieth centuries; he was one of the few Jewish thinkers of
his time affected more by English and French than by German
sources. The decisive factor, however, was his belief that the
strong attachment of historic Judaism to ethics rather than
religious belief was sufficient to ensure the historical continuity
of Judaism. Singling out ethics as the basic ingredient of Judaism,
Ahad Ha-am would emphasize the importance of prophetic
Judaism, more rooted in ethics than in faith proper, in the
historical development of Jewish thought throughout the ages.

One of the ways in which Ahad Ha-am justified his emphasis
on ethics was by comparing the Jewish and Christian attitudes
towards the subject. Judaism is concerned more with social than

with individual ethics, and it holds society responsible for the realization of ethical imperatives in the social sphere. Judaism lays stress on objective justice, not on love and compassion. Judaism judges the deed, not the doer; it does this according to a fixed, objective standard and not, as with Christianity, in the light of subjective motives or the promptings of the human heart. Obviously, social justice and social ethics are closely related in Judaism, the first being in fact the realization and implementation of the second.[1]

We can thus understand Ahad Ha-am's elite, which identifies itself with the fate of the people, as representing a realization of the ethical content of Judaism. The ultimate purpose of the Jewish revival, indeed, is the revival of Jewish ethics. But the condition for this revival is implicit in each Jew's willingness to adhere to these ethics here and now, that is to say, to give priority to the people as an entity over the fate of the individual. Ahad Ha-am distinguishes between essence and its manifestations. The essence of Judaism is ethics, a system of norms which can be preserved in the modern world and to which all Jews can give their allegiance. The manifestations of Judaism, including the religious one, change in the course of history.

IT WAS AHAD HA-AM'S CONSTANT AIM to discern the line of the historical continuity that joined the present to the past. Although he formulated his thoughts on this subject at various times, they are most fully elaborated in two essays: "Moses"[2] and "Flesh and Spirit" (*Bassar Varuah*),[3] published in the third volume of his work *At the Crossroads* (*Al Parashat Drakhim*).

Ahad Ha-am's views on Zionism and culture may be seen as a kind of genealogical tree whose highest point is prophecy. The essence of the prophetic conception, according to Ahad Ha-am, is its synthesis of political and ethical elements. Too great an emphasis upon either leads to extremism or one-sidedness.

Undue stress upon the political factor in the life of society, an over-concern with day-to-day affairs, constitutes for Ahad

Ha-am political materialism. An excessive emphasis on ethics, so that it is torn from its context in the day-to-day life of the people, is a "killing the flesh," an asceticism transferred from the realm of the individual to that of society. The prophets are the bearers of the total national ideals, and their constant aim is the realization of those ideals in the life of the people. Without a vital social ethic, life becomes stale and futile — and a deviation from the teachings of the prophets of Israel.

The prophetic viewpoint is used by Ahad Ha-am (in "Flesh and Spirit") as a criterion by which to measure historical phenomena and institutions. He sees in the institutions of kingship and the court in Biblical times an archetype of the political factor triumphant, a tendency which would be revived later under different conditions by the Sadducees. In the Essenes, who despised politics and led a life of ethical purity removed from social reality, he finds the prototype of the ascetic, or what we may call the spiritualistic (as opposed to the materialistic) deviation in Jewish history. The assimilationist movements in Judaism in the nineteenth century appear to him as modern versions of this tendency to shun political life, indeed to offer it as a sacrifice on the altar of an abstract ethical ideal. Israel then becomes a spirit without a body. Spirituality becomes not only the aim but the sole content of Jewish life. The flesh — the Jewish people as an entity — is to the assimilationist not only something subsidiary but actually dangerous, a hindrance to the development of the spirit and its conquest of the world.

It is not our purpose here to evaluate the correctness of this historical analysis but rather the implications that Ahad Ha-am drew from it. He criticized political Zionism (in "Flesh and Spirit") as only the most recent manifestation of the materialistic tendency in Jewish history, as a case of an extreme view — that is, assimilationism — producing its opposite (as, he noted, extreme views always do) in a vision of Israel confined to its "body," to the Jewish state alone.[4] This is a clear, deliberately formulated rather than polemical statement of Ahad Ha-am's position on political Zionism and its place in history. If the goal of the assimilationists was the life of the spirit only, and to this end they were prepared to sacrifice the social and national integrity of the Jewish community, the political Zionists were willing to jettison Jewish cultural values in the interest of political unity. In the larger historical perspective, political Zionism was a recrudescence of the materialism of the royal court and the Sadducees, and a life-view inimical to prophecy and the prophetic spirit.

Over and against these extremes Ahad Ha-am posited a belief whose source he saw in prophecy and whose visions he found embodied in Pharisaic Judaism: cultural Zionism. Past experience, he said, shows that both assimilationism and political Zionism, having no firm hold upon the heart of the people, will disappear and give place to the only belief that can command their full allegiance, that promulgated by the Prophets in the days of the first state and by the Pharisees in the second. "If, as we hope, there is to be a third [Jewish state], its fundamental principle, on the national as on the individual plane, will be neither the ascendancy of the body over the spirit, nor the suppression of the body for the spirit's sake, but the uplifting of the body by the spirit."[5]

A well-known passage at the end of his essay "Moses" relates Ahad Ha-am's thinking to a millennial tradition:

> The Cabbalists have well said that Moses is rein-carnated in every age.
> The prophetic spirit does not remain in abeyance for long; it soon reasserts its hold on the recalcitrant prophet. So, too, the prophetic people was brought to heel and restored to self-consciousness. And once again we see in faint outline the reincarnation of Moses, and the same Spirit that summoned him thousands of years ago and sent him all unwilling on his mission, repeats its imperious summons to our generation at this moment: "And that which cometh into your mind shall not be at all; in that ye say: We will be as the nations . . . As I live, saith the

Lord God, surely with a mighty hand . . . will I be king over you."[6]

Here God Himself seems to stand against political Zionism, whose program in a sense was to create a nation like other nations, and to demand a more spiritual kind of commonwealth. The name *Bnei Moshe* (Society of Sons of Moses) that Ahad Ha-am gave the organization he founded as a kind of Order, contained the idea of a reincarnation of the spirit of Moses, master of the prophets, and served to imbue its members with a feeling of sacred purpose.

AHAD HA-AM'S CONCEPTION embraced not only the relationship between the ethical and the political aspects of Judaism but also that between the individual and society with regard to the goal of human existence. In the Biblical literature of the classical prophetic period, this goal was taken to be the preservation of the communal life, which in turn was considered to exist for the fulfillment in practical life of the ethical values whose bearer it was. According to Ahad Ha-am, prophetic Judaism does not aspire to an equal fusion of society and the individual, but rather to a synthesis which favors the former, which he conceived to be more basic and comprehensive.

It is not our purpose to enlarge on this theme, except to point out how Ahad Ha-am related his idea (though not explicitly) to the original sources and to the basic outlook of Judaism. As noted previously, he criticized Hibbath Zion and especially political Zionism for failing to put the Jewish people as a whole at the center of Zionist aspirations, and for neglecting to establish the vital ties that unite the individual Jew with the national revival of the Jewish people. In "This Is Not the Way" (*Lo Zeh Ha-Derekh*) Ahad Ha-am declares that he is unable to understand how the "language of self-interest" which speaks to each individual according to his own status and ambitions can be called to serve in place of the national sentiment which unites all hearts in a common purpose. As between the individual and society, he held that the latter was both more important and more efficacious in its appeal.

It is obvious that even in the practical realm Ahad Ha-am was working in what he believed to be the tradition of the prophets. Indeed, he asserted that the ethical idea of prophecy was sufficient to give the Jewish revival its impulse and content. Cultural Zionism, which for him was the solution to the real problem of Judaism, merely meant a return to the ethical ideas of the religion of the Bible. In other words, the generation of the revival, which had been enjoined to identify itself with the entire people, need only follow the ethical imperatives of the prophets in order to achieve its goal. Thus Ahad Ha-am tried to merge the national impulse with traditional thought.

The emphasis on the individual which finds expression in Biblical Judaism in the books of Ezekiel and Job was interpreted by Ahad Ha-am as a departure from the authentic ethical principle in Judaism. In "This Is Not the Way" he states that the Jews began to complain about the fate of "the righteous man who perishes in his righteousness" only when the common weal failed to inspire them and to lift up their hearts. Men then discovered a private life apart from that of society, a life whose purpose was pleasure and contentment and in which righteousness was rewarded. Ahad Ha-am saw the rise of the individual as the result of the decline of a society which could no longer satisfy his aspirations. A parallel analysis is found in Hermann Cohen's conception of the prophetic ideal as based on society and the people as a whole. The book of Ezekiel, with its emphasis on the individual, his sins and repentance, represents in Cohen's view also a departure from tradition. But this shift of the center of ethical and religious consciousness to the individual was interpreted by Cohen, in contrast to Ahad Ha-am, as a progressive development and not as a falling away. [7]

The difference in the outlook of these two thinkers is particularly evident here. Ahad Ha-am, who was interested in the existence and revival of a united Jewish people, interprets the emergence of individualism as a weakening of the social structure. Cohen, concerned with the religious ideals of Judaism, tends to minimize, ignore and even despise national goals and stresses the spiritual position of the individual in Judaism. For Ahad Ha-am the enduring content of Judaism is determined by its early social origin; for Cohen it is determined by the later refinement of religious consciousness, placing in the central position the individual, his sin and repentance.

WHAT WAS IT that prompted Ahad Ha-am to seek the origin of cultural Zionism in prophecy? Ahad Ha-am did not look upon Zionism as a new movement; to him it was the highest expression of the ancient desire of the Jewish people to re-create its national existence and to preserve its unity under the social conditions of the age. Ahad Ha-am's thinking is permeated by a basic assumption that the existence of the people rests upon a tacit covenant made by the generations with one another. A people's existence, he holds, cannot be explained in terms of its present attributes alone, and by this token the Jews' desire to establish a sovereign state is based on an active corporate will nourished by a consciousness of the past. Ahad Ha-am's nationalism shows little of the positivism that was so dominant in other areas of his thinking. Its ideological roots were deepest in German Romanticism, and it bears resemblance to the political thought of Adam Müller, although without the latter's mysticism and irrationalism. According to Ahad Ha-am, the irresistible and all-pervading force of history has its source in the past. The spirit of nationality owes its being to this power, which is constant and which in Judaism is fed by the spirit of Biblical prophecy.

Ahad Ha-am believed that behind the covenant of the generations lay a profound consciousness of Biblical Judaism, a consciousness that bound the generations to one another and united them by virtue of a common source.* It should be remembered that one of the basic ideas of the Jewish Enlightenment was that of the Bible as the ideal image of the life of Israel. This romantic view of Scripture in the rationalistic circles of the *Haskalah* also tended to modify Ahad Ha-am's positivistic outlook.

Ahad Ha-am did not find it necessary to inquire into the historical factors behind the continuous Jewish prophetic tradition, although he was wont to use historical labels. He was basically concerned with psychological characteristics, as we see in "Moses," where he most clearly set forth his ideas of the prophet and his mission. The prophet, he held, is not to be viewed as a concrete personality responding to a unique historical situation, but rather a type defined by general qualities—"a man of truth," "a man of extremes," and the like. These qualities are characterological ones, and they do not refer to actual ideas, to God's active intervention in human history or to the responsibility of the individual and the people to God. Thus Ahad Ha-am deprives the image of the prophet of its theistic, or faith, element, and disregards the dependence of individuals or the people on the laws laid down by the divine legislator. Ahad Ha-am's commitment to the modernist conception explains his neglect of the content and substance of prophecy. Here he clearly modernizes traditional ideas to enable modern man to cling to tradition. If the prophet is not an apostle with a heavenly mission, designated by God to act as a "channel" between Him and the people, that function is reserved to the priest. The prophet is moved by an inner imperative, by a vision of faith beyond human control. By turning prophecy into a psychological category, Ahad Ha-am sought to establish the genealogy of spiritual Zionism. His position was not unlike that of medieval Jewish philosophy, which also regarded prophecy as a "natural" phenomenon

* Ahad Ha-am differs with the Orthodox view which derives the historical continuity of the generations from the Written and Oral Law alone and eschews any additional external impulse.

conditioned by individual psychology. It differed from the latter, however, in two respects: the medieval philosophers did not separate prophecy from traditional faith, and they placed Moses beyond the limits of natural phenomena—as it were, in a class by himself.

IN HIS DESIRE to find a historical basis for his ideas and to clarify the issues of his own generation, Ahad Ha-am read his own modern views into the early history of prophecy. But he was unable to resolve satisfactorily the problem of continuation or renewal, or of the continuation that is at the same time a renewal. His ideas relating to the historical events of his age shed some light on this question.

Ahad Ha-am's views on the forces that shape history and the sources that nourish national experience have been pointedly analyzed by Yehezkel Kaufmann. Kaufmann pinpointed biology as the prime factor in Ahad Ha-am's thinking about history and society.[8] The people is a social organism which is animated and sustained by the elementary instinct for preservation and survival. On close examination this instinct presents two aspects: the biological urge to continue existing through time and the response to menace—individual or collective—at any point. The menace may be direct, as in open persecution, or subtle, as in acculturation, but in either case the healthy organism will recognize it and deal with it.

Kaufmann frequently refers to a phrase which Ahad Ha-am took from biology when analyzing the dynamic character of Jewish history: "the urge to survive." It is difficult to prove, however, that Ahad Ha-am used the phrase in its purely biological sense, or else regarded the urge to survive as the predominant factor in history. It seems to have served Ahad Ha-am as a common name for a number of forces that are not necessarily, or not entirely, biological.

Ahad Ha-am defined the urge to survive in a very general

sense as "an inner force that bolsters national feeling" and as "the will of the generations." This suggests factors in the life of the people which are at once biological, cultural and social. Specifically, "the will of the generations" implies a force that is more historical than biological in origin and essence, or one that does not precede history but is created and formed through it.

Furthermore, the urge to survive exhibits a curious dialectic in its development, often using for its purpose doctrines that are clearly contradictory. For example, the doctrine of assimilation and the doctrine that makes of Jewish nationality a purely religious idea could both be instruments of the urge to survive, either explicitly or else disguised in other forms. Since both these doctrines deny Jewish national cohesion, they seem to negate the will to survive as a people proper. But they make—nilly and not willy—for the preservation of Jewish national existence within a definite historical, social and ideological setting. Through the "cunning of reason," the dialectic of the urge to survive converts apparently destructive forces into constructive and preservative ones. Thus the relationship between means and ends is neither simple nor unambiguous. It entails distinctions between the visible will of the advocates of assimilation, the biological entity of the assimilationists themselves, and the hidden will of the generations behind it—a historical phenomenon clearly not rooted in biology. So we see that even when Ahad Ha-am employs biological terminology he may have non-biological considerations in mind.

THE TRUTH IS that there was no single unifying principle governing Ahad Ha-am's thinking. His analysis of historical forces and the role of the individual in society contains a number of diverse elements, which the fragmentary character of his writings cannot alone account for. We must look, rather, to the principles of historicism, prevalent in his day, which sought to explain all phenomena in terms of their historical roots and necessarily resulted in a system which was inconsistent and without unity. Ahad Ha-am requires dialectical explanations and laws deriving from positivistic sociology to give his thinking purpose and order, just as he requires strictly biological explanations. The important thing for him is not the manner of historical development but the development itself. He sees the drama of man's aspiration as more than a record or mere events, as the unfolding of the *Volksgeist*, the Genius of the national soul. Man is not an isolated phenomenon, he affirmed, but the product of particular circumstances of time and place, custom and tradition.

YET AHAD HA-AM SHARED A TENDENCY to regard values in an isolated state, separate from the time process. Although in his view it is from history that absolute, eternal values emerged, they eventually detached themselves from it in time and became independent and ahistorical. The historical process, so to speak, overflowed its banks and left a deposit that was no longer subject to its movement. When Ahad Ha-am speaks of national character as determined by history, he has in mind two distinct things: national character as formed in history but also as leading its own independent existence. The historical conception helps him describe the various stages in the development of values, but it does not prevent him from seeing these values as independent, their validity eventually unaffected by their development in time. This dualistic approach makes for a distinction between source and validity, the former being rooted in history and the latter placed in an absolute normative sphere.

However, we must not ignore the anti-historical elements in Ahad Ha-am's thinking, particularly his view that the sources of values may lie outside of history. The idea of God, for example, is prior to any historical process and entered history from without. Judaism, as Ahad Ha-am understood it, is an attempt to raise the religious and ethical consciousness above every finite form of sensibility and attach it to an abstract ideal. Hence it is explicitly defined as a system that divorces values from their development in time. To the extent that Ahad Ha-am takes certain values to be absolute from the standpoint of their source and validity, his conception must be considered to be anti-historical—or normative in the sense that these values represent norms which by virtue of their eternality lay claim to our allegiance.

Ahad Ha-am bases his normative position on the history of Judaism. No less than medieval Jewish philosophers, the historicists of the nineteenth century looked upon the Jewish religion as an absolute value. This conception held the Jewish people to be involved in a nationality whose values could not be challenged without jeopardy to its very existence. The national movement, which by its very nature was a link in the historical chain, must therefore be considered as an attempt to reformulate and preserve absolute values. This would seem to be the precise meaning of "renaissance."

THE STRUGGLE BETWEEN THESE TWO TENDENCIES in Ahad Ha-am's thinking may be interpreted as a reflection of the absence of system in his philosophy. His views, however, were not born *in vacuo* but arose from a clearly defined national movement which also struggled with the problem of reconciling these differences. If the national movement represented an attempt to add a new dimension to Jewish existence, to forge a new link in the chain of historical tradition, it may be regarded as also looking to a return to the source. That is to say, the driving force of a renewed nationalism is at times seen as directed toward a restoration or revival—an interpretation, moreover, which is not foreign to the essential meaning of the movement. If this urge to nationalism is directed to the source, it possesses at the very outset a goal that can be pursued inflexibly by its adherents. Thus the very nature of the Jewish national movement—which was seen both as a historical development and a repository of eternal values—imparted to Ahad Ha-am's thinking its characteristic dual quality. To be sure, such a contradiction at the heart of his thinking is less than satisfactory, but his presentation and reformulation of the problems that engaged the best Jewish minds of the nineteenth and twentieth centuries is, unquestionably, an achievement of lasting importance.

Ahad Ha-am's statement of the inherent problems seems therefore, more significant than their attempted solution. As a solution his thinking is more of a compromise than a synthesis.

CHAPTER SEVEN

Cultural Ingathering

WITH BIALIK we come full circle back to the ideas of the founders of the Science of Judaism—but with an essential difference. To the latter, the treasures of Jewish creativity endured as the remains of a culture that had reached its terminus. To Bialik, they comprised the most valuable possession of a living people and a guide to their intact survival and future creativity.

Haim Nahman Bialik was born in a small village in Volhynia, Russia, in 1873. When he was seven years old, his father died, and he was sent to live with his grandfather, a man of learning and extreme piety. As a youth at the Yeshiva of Volozhin, Bialik became caught up in the fervor of contemporary problems, publishing an article on colonization in Palestine, as well as his first poem, in his early twenties. But he found the Yeshiva oppressive and moved to Odessa; here he met and received encouragement from Ahad Ha-am. His first volume of poems was brought out in 1901. In 1905 he founded the distinguished Hebrew publishing house "Moriah," whose success gave him the leisure to pursue his writing career. In time, he came to be regarded as the greatest Hebrew poet of his day, the laureate of the Jewish renaissance. Following the Russian Revolution, he continued to champion the cause of Hebrew language and culture and fell into disfavor with the Soviet authorities. Through the intercession of Maxim Gorki, he was allowed to leave Russia in 1921. He settled in Tel Aviv in 1924, where Ahad Ha-am had come three years earlier, and lived there for the remaining decade of his life.

AGAINST THE BACKGROUND of the Jewish renaissance and the movement to create through Zionism a Jewish society, it was inevitable that a concern with culture would arise. We have seen the importance of this theme for Ahad Ha-am. In Bialik too, culture is the central concept.

However, Bialik's observation that a people's culture comprises all forms of its life, from the lowest to the highest, cannot be taken for his characteristic point of view.[1] He was primarily concerned with what he termed "the highest forms" of culture. These he conceived as the sum-total of all the expresssions of a people's creative powers, manifest in its social mores and institutions on the one hand, and in its literature, in the broadest sense, on the other. Bialik looked upon culture both as a national treasure and as a spiritual reservoir; it was the fruit of the people's experience which through time had become enriched in meaning.[2] Because it was rooted in an ancient heritage and also symbolized that heritage, it was tightly and inseparably interwoven with the people's collective life.

The distinguishing mark of Bialik's conception of culture is the central position he assigns to the legacy of past generations. This is why Bialik's discussions of cultural questions are dominated by a conviction that history is an essential part of culture. It may be said, in fact, that the historicity of culture is the dominant motif running through Bialik's thought.

From the viewpoint of human creation, he regarded culture as an amalgam of man's intentions, opinions, thoughts, desires and expressions of will, as well as the gifts of heaven and nature.[3] Culture was primarily a manifestation of intention, of man's power of self-determination. It comprised, as it were, the molds in which man's will and the rules by which he regulated his conduct were configured. Thus, if we seek to determine the future direction of a people's cultural life, we need to understand its past, since by its very nature that life is voluntary and self-channeling. To put it pointedly, Bialik's treatment of culture revolves around the twin ideas of volition and regulation, and the problem that concerns him is how to bring these qualities to light—to the level of consciousness and direction.

BEFORE PROCEEDING to a detailed analysis of Bialik's views, it behooves us to look at his conceptual framework. Bialik believed that in the consciousness of the Jewish people the secular idea of culture had taken the place of the theology-centered one of Torah.[4] He himself was involved in this shift. Though he conceived of culture as rooted in the past, still he did not challenge either the direction in which it had developed or the dethronement of theology which this development entailed. And Bialik does not seem to have questioned at any time the legitimacy of the heir-apparent.

Indeed, Bialik regarded historical trends as irresistible and believed voluntary self-regulation to be subject to historical circumstances and currents. No will in the world can resist nature, Bialik thought—"nature" connoting here the sum-total of given circumstances. The will has decisive weight only when it is in harmony with historical tendencies, and in any contest with history the will must fail.[5] It is the spirit, or genius, of the time which has determinative force. The very idea of the overthrow of religious tradition in favor of culture reflects a historical-spiritual movement with which Bialik could not but make his peace. Thus, in dealing with the dominant current of thought of his day, Bialik sought to ride with, rather than check, its flow. The finality of Bialik's acceptance of history ought not to surprise us, even when we recall the ambivalence towards it in some of his poetry. For, clearly, the rules of systematic thought are more conducive to unequivocal statements than are the imaginative license and depths of the creative process. So far as Bialik as thinker was concerned, it was his intellectual and psychic acknowledgment of the historical trend of his day which determined the major tenets of his views on culture, and particularly on the future of Jewish culture.

ONCE—SAYS BIALIK—RELIGION REIGNED SUPREME; now that its sway is ending, we must gather everything into the folds of one language, a language which represents our family tree.[6] Bialik raises the Hebrew language to the rank of a national legacy which embodies and crystallizes the transition from religion to culture and constitutes a replacement for the religious norms in previous generations. Where he asserts that "the heart of peoplehood is embodied in form,"[7] he is merely putting this transition more pointedly.

Bialik's formalism, which is likely to surprise those who are acquainted only with his poetry, is frequently encountered in his theoretical consideration of national problems. In one place he traces his position to the twelfth-century philosopher Yehuda Halevi, whose views, he insists, resemble his own.[8] Thus, according to Bialik, Yehuda Halevi assigned cardinal value to the form of religion, land, language and commandments. Yet Bialik entertains some doubts as to the power of language as form to perpetuate and further the people's cultural existence, and these doubts lead him sometimes towards a more comprehensive view. "Woe unto that people which bases everything on language alone . . .," he exclaims. "Happily for us, language too is but a part." Nevertheless, he did not take the position that Hebrew was but a phase of the religious heritage, the form sanctified as carrier of religious doctrine. Rather, he saw it as the sap and fiber of national existence, rooted in the soil in its most literal sense—the Land of Israel.

To Bialik's mind, what distinguishes language from all other components of a national legacy is its organic, indissoluble unity with the life of the people. The category of radical change does not apply to language. Its content may change, but not the language itself; it only undergoes development.[9] Thus, in addition to the conventional distinction between content and form, we find in Bialik the assertion of a unique inner relation between language and the men and women who use it, a relation which, moreover, entails its own self-preservation. "The language and the nation, so to speak, are the growth and the grower,"[10] he declares metaphorically. One can no more separate peoplehood from the possession of a common, national tongue than one can separate growth from the thing growing.

As he moved away from a strictly formal conception of language towards an organic one, Bialik naturally came to emphasize the historical aspects of language. From a formal point of View, there is no need to examine, let alone stress, these aspects. We must create and fashion within the language, he says, and thus elevate it to the level of a holy tongue—but we can do so only if we do not banish all those spirits which have inhabited the language during thousands of years.[11] Even though the precise meaning of "holy" in this context is far from clear—and perhaps the ambiguity is intentional—Bialik is certainly declaring a bond with the past. In another passage he says that behind every true language, in prose and poetry, stands the speech of the forefathers, "a host of distant echoes."[12]

Bialik's shifting from a formal to an organic treatment of the function of language may reflect his essentially dialectical view of the renascence of the Jewish people. The more he stresses the formal aspects of language, the more he seems to realize that, precisely in its status as a form, the Hebrew language is not exhausted. This same status is but the reverse side of its historical character, of its being rooted in the entire history of the people. Because it reaches back into the past, language is the medium in and through which the connection with the world of bygone generations is maintained. This bond itself is not direct but mediated through language. It entails no acknowledgment of the past as a binding norm but only a continuing awareness and responsiveness to the past's enduring content. Basically, Bialik is interested in preserving the past in the consciousness of the present, rather than in forging a deeper, more intimate relation with it. In a tradition-permeated language he sees a guarantee — automatic as well as deliberate — that the creations of old will be preserved in those of the present and future.

BIALIK'S AFFIRMATION OF HISTORICAL TRENDS, on the one hand, and his view that these must be regulated deliberately, on the other, form the ultimate support of his project of ingathering (*kinus*) the creations of Jewish genius down through the ages, and of his vision of the Jewish culture of the future, nurtured once more on the native ground of the land of Israel. In proclaiming a "time of ingathering"[13] Bialik called for an organized attempt to republish or make available again the chief documents of Jewish literary creation through all the ages. Yet underlying this practical program were considerations of a historical and ideological character which deserve pointing out.

Bialik insisted that he was not simply putting forward his own individual program but rather that he was giving voice to a drive immanent in the heart of the people throughout its history. The sources of this drive were psychological as well as historical. The major difference between the present and the past, he said, was that his generation had made explicit what had before been implicit as twin characteristics of the national soul in an age-long process of successive materialization: two immutable tendencies, the one toward outgoingness and expansion, the other longing for ingathering and singularity.[14] The inner rhythm of these two psychological forces he found in harmony with the goals of the present. The physical or sociopolitical process of territorial ingathering in the Land of Israel was paralleled, so to speak, by the spiritual enterprise of assembling the people's treasures scattered throughout the world. There were, in fact, several levels of meaning implicit in Bialik's conception of ingathering.

In speaking of "the essential characteristic of ingathering"[15] Bialik meant to imply that behind the project lay more than was apparent on the surface—an elemental force that revealed itself in all aspects of the social history of the people. Bialik even went so far as to apply the expression "ingathering of the exiles" to the cultural dispersion.[16] The analogy between the physical and the spiritual is even closer in the case of the parallel ideas of the Land of Israel as a spiritual center (which Bialik took over from Ahad Ha-am) and the ingathering of the people's spiritual creations. Here, however, it was obviously impossible to identify the somewhat technical process entailed in the latter with the all-encompassing reality of the former. But the fact that Bialik viewed them as related can be seen in his call to Jewry in the Land of Israel to shoulder the task of assembling, and thus preserving, the treasures of the people, otherwise doomed to extinction day by day and hour by hour.[17] Bialik explicitly referred to the idea of rescuing Judaism—which, as we have seen, was the cornerstone of Ahad Ha-am's thought—and applied it in a restricted sense to the saving of the great works of Jewish creativity. In drawing his analogies, Bialik sought to establish a common denominator of historical processes and forces and to show that these would direct Jewry in Eretz Israel. The culture to be created would constitute an explicit, concentrated crystallization of a primal Jewish historical tendency. This idea of a collective effort brings us to another aspect of Bialik's alignment with historical trends, though one which Bialik himself failed to develop as fully as might be desired.

In dealing with classical Hebrew or Judaic literature, Bialik usually emphasized its collective and even anonymous character. In contradistinction to the literature of ancient Israel, that of the Diaspora bears, according to Bialik, the stamp of its individual

authors.[18] It must have caused Bialik, the most individual of
poets, no small pain to point out that individuality in art is out
of tune with the character of classical Jewish creation, that personality is, as it were, one of the expressions of the Diaspora.*
The ingathering project obviously could not be deemed to be
anonymous so far as its execution was concerned. Still, it would
bear no personal mark, since its realization presupposed the
effort of many people and was impossible on the basis of spurious
individual attempts. In a sense, one might say that the dawn of
Jewish history finds its counterpart in this late stage of Jewish
history, as Bialik foresaw it. The undertaking was in basic
harmony with the spirit of the Land of Israel which, as the
saying goes, if it does not make us any wiser, yet arouses the
collective spirit. Bialik was consciously following in the footsteps
of scholarly predecessors, who likewise had made compilations
of the works of former generations, as a continuing literary
process, which had its beginning with the Bible.

From a psychological point of view, the very bond with
history, presupposed as well as effected by the ingathering,
bears witness to a guilty national conscience. The project would
express the will of the people "as long as in its heart it felt
itself responsible for saving its treasures, living and dead."[19]
The distinction between living and dead treasures is an important
one for Bialik and implies the need for a selection, one which will
favor the living over the dead. But Bialik does not wish to sever
connections with the bygone world. He has come, as it were, to
distill the past, not to bury it. Still, if the past is to be preserved,
it must be rid of those of its aspects which are no more than
ballast. There is a need for a final reckoning with the burden the
people continues to shoulder, as long as its sense of responsibility
is still inchoate, still awaiting crystallization and channeling
in a fully conscious ingathering. This vague yet insistent feeling,
bordering on guilt towards the past, calls for relief by way of an

---

* Compare the views of Ahad Ha-am and Hermann Cohen on the individual
versus the collectivity in the preceding chapter.

elucidation of the desirable relation between the present and the past.

One outcome of a reckoning with the past would be the birth of a new creativity. Bialik says that the sole purpose of the assemblage is to expand the sphere of influence of the literature still to be written.[20] In other words, the selective gathering will set a seal on the legacy of former times. Then the past will no longer constitute an oppressive weight, as it does now, precisely because it is bequeathed in its entirety and assigned an unqualified ancestral dignity.

Yet it is not only to lighten the load of the past, and thus disencumber the present, that the ingathering must be selective, but also to guide the present towards accepting, rather than rebelling against, the past. The ingathering must break down barriers and create a unity between old and new, so that the two are fused without impediment.[21] Bialik is not clear as to how the selective process will effect this union, unless it involves some kind of reactivation of the old, including a reinstatement of its normative value for the present. Yet whether a revival of the past to this degree was intended by Bialik is a moot question, since he never really distinguished between the technical import of his project as an inventory and its profounder significance as a reflection of a cultural renascence. In essence, according to Bialik, every renaissance is but a return to the origins by a new and short route, the latest revolution of an old wheel. But Bialik seems to have been unable to cope with the dialectical nature of renaissance, which is always Janus-faced: one aspect turned towards the old, the other towards the new.

IT MAY BE AS AN ENDEAVOR to resolve the ambivalence of the relation of the present to the past—an ambivalence immanent in the very notion of ingathering—that Bialik frequently characterized the past as the fostering soil of the present.[22] "It is not a question of the old," he says, "but rather a question of soil for the generation of a new culture." In another passage he remarks: "Even the spiritual world sends its roots into the soil."[23] This, of course, does not get us very far, since there is a world of difference between an acknowledgment of the normative author- ity of the past and its exploitation as, say, a fertile point of departure for creativity in the present. For Bialik, the value of the past lies in its inexhaustibility. There will always be material for the creative process because "the soil is never consumed, nor does it age." But the eternality of the soil does not demand our constant awareness; it is what feeds and grows upon the soil that we see and appreciate. In Bialik, the accent remains on the present, though he does attempt to harmonize the antithetical tendencies—loyalty to the past and a yearning for rebirth— both of which are essential and germane to a national renaissance.

Although Bialik criticized the idea of a "Treasure of Judaism" (*Otzar Ha-yahadut*) put forward by Ahad Ha-am in an attempt to isolate the core of Jewish creativity, his presentation of cultural problems and his suggested solutions were obviously dominated by the influence of Ahad Ha-am, so much so that it would not be wrong to include Bialik among Ahad Ha-am's followers. Yet we must remember that Bialik's were modest or minimal pro- posals. Unlike Ahad Ha-am, Bialik does not essay to raise the content of traditional Judaism (for example, Judaic ethics in the Ahad Ha-amian sense of the term) to the rank of a normative value. He considers it sufficient to assemble the source materials of Judaism and to expect no more than an acknowledgment of their generative potentiality. He is more inclined to take stock than to care for the continuation of a set of beliefs or norms.

THE PRESENT AND FUTURE STAGES of culture are not limited by the past upon which they feed. But in describing the nature of the new creations that will spring out of the soil of the past, Bialik is vague, to say the least. There is one matter, however,

to which he attributes central importance and gives much
thought, especially in his essay on "Jewish Law and Lore"
("*Halakhah Ve-aggadah*"), namely, the need to establish traditional law as a component of the people's cultural life. For
Bialik, the legal code of *Halakhah* represents a firm, solid framework diametrically opposed to spontaneous innovation. This
explains the paradoxical twist which he gave to the Zionist ideal
of an earthly national existence.

The status of traditional law was a central bone of contention
in nineteenth-century Jewish thought and Hebrew literature, and
the criticism of tradition was essentially a criticism of *Halakhah*.
In this matter Bialik differed from the thinking of his time by
evaluating the Talmud not as a negation of human emotion or,
as some said, the embodiment of casuistry and sophism, but
rather as a constructive restraint. To Bialik, the Talmud as a
codified body of traditional law represented a call to a way of
life. Here again, Bialik the thinker overshadows Bialik the poet
and finds the solidity of fixed molds preferable to the liberty of
creative ventures. Significantly, in his appreciation of Ahad
Ha-am, Bialik asserts that the great force of the man's teaching
lay in his demand for an orderly, well-defined way of life, though
it is debatable if Ahad Ha-am makes a clear call for a strict social
discipline. One might describe Bialik's viewpoint in this matter
as spiritual realism based upon the principles of the established
Halakhic regulative authority. This carries over to his thinking
on language, whose power, he asserts, lies in its status as a
creation to be taken for granted. That is, language is a component
of culture which exists *ab initio* as a matter of course, and as such
constitutes a regulative factor.

As an individual creator, Bialik sees the hackneyed linguistic
form as concealing outworn emotions; as a thinker concerned
with culture and society, he regards the customary mold as
part of the objective existence of the collectivity and regards it
as binding by virtue of its soundness and historicity.

IN A SENSE, Bialik's thought epitomizes the whole history of modern Jewish ideas. Bialik does not pretend to solve the problem of tradition. Indeed, he consciously avoids any fixed solution by regarding the present stage of Jewish history as transitional only. While various nineteenth-century thinkers believed they had laid the problem to rest, Bialik could not entertain such an illusion. Yet, acknowledging his perplexity, he kept the door open. He called upon his generation to know the past first, selective as that knowledge might be. Knowledge of the past might power a new wave of creativity; it might also be no more than a summation.

Where does the open door lead? The last part of this volume will be devoted to that question.

PART FOUR

The Problematic Situation of the Present

CHAPTER EIGHT

Reformulating Ideas

WHAT WE HAVE SEEN in all of the thinkers whose ideas we have considered, from Zunz through Bialik, is the effect of a reinterpretation of the concept of Jewish tradition, which had come to be understood as something primarily identical with the historical process of the Jews' religious heritage. Considered in previous generations a binding norm because it was rooted in revelation, the tradition had come to be viewed by these thinkers as the sum total of changes it had undergone, together with existent customs and opinions. If it was to serve as a guide to behavior, this would be in accordance with new norms, or even norms that were different from those of tradition itself.

In large part, the impetus behind this new way of looking at tradition was social and economic. In the nineteenth and twentieth centuries, Jews were given opportunities that had been denied them for centuries, to live their lives among different peoples and cultures and to become an integral part of their host environments. The ideological formulations of the times tended to make these opportunities more accessible, whether they were welcomed or rejected, but at a certain price. A concept of tradition that testifies to the changes that have taken place within Judaism and opens the way for further changes by denying the norms that provide men with imperatives is, in the end, destructive of tradition as a vital governing force.

But during the time of change with which we have been dealing, the question of norms was never absent from Jewish thought. Confronted with the possibility of striking roots in non-Jewish cultures and enjoying their advantages, Jews always remained concerned with preserving their identity as Jews in terms of a tradition which linked them together. The proposed solutions covered a wide range of attempts and attitudes, and some of the more important formulations are worthy of notice.

The first of these proposed solutions is modern Orthodoxy. The Orthodox do not deny the existence of other nations and cultures. Even Samson Raphael Hirsch accepted the fact of historical changes—except that he considered these as occurring outside the bounds of the Jewish people. The Jews, as Hirsch viewed them, were exempt from the historical process because the religious truth imparted to them anteceded that process.[1] If history, in Lessing's phrase, is "the education of the human race," it applies only to peoples that are without Torah. While Israel lives among such peoples and in their cultures, it absorbs some things which are external to the Torah and its authentic meaning. But the worldly life of Jews (*derekh eretz*), encompassing their day-to-day life and its needs outside the inner world of Torah, is not detrimental to the latter because it is impervious to change. From Hirsch's point of view, the relationship between Jews and Torah is not comparable with the relationship between other peoples of the world and *derekh eretz*; the Jews dwell outside the stream of history and the others within it. Relationships between Jews and other peoples are basically tangential and do not affect the metaphysical essence of the Jews.

This denial of historical experience to Jews, however, presents several kinds of problems. It assumes that there can be a union of Torah and *derekh eretz*, albeit a superficial and mechanical one, that does not influence the content of Torah. It rests on a view of history that must be managed in such a way that the inner life of Judaism always remains untouched. The Orthodox wishes to maintain that the Jewish norm is not to be found in history, and that that which is given in history does not fall within the province of the norm. But the separation he creates is in effect a compromise, and one that makes no philosophical distinction between the essential and the non-historical. An Orthodox Jew prays — as it were — outside the world in which he actually lives, and then returns to this world to which his prayers do not pertain.

There are religious movements in modern Judaism which acknowledge historical changes, but which nevertheless seek to establish limits in one direction or another. The various currents of Reform Judaism, as well as — to some extent at least — those of the Conservative Movement, particularly in the United States, are committed to this view. The problem they face in common is where to draw the line on innovation.

Reform Judaism is inclined to seek the limits of change in the lofty ethics of prophetic Judaism, the idea of an ethical universe, the principle that all men as children of their heavenly father constitute one humanity, or a vision of the reign of ethics throughout the world. These religious, intellectual or philosophical assumptions constitute, for Reform Jews, the ultimate core of Judaism. This core is not subject to change, although its expressions have changed in the past and continue to change in the present, as they should properly do. For what we have here within a dynamic tradition is a constant factor which influences change and is influenced by it, and which nevertheless has an ultimate normative significance for humanity and Judaism alike. Insofar as ideas have universal meaning, they influence tradition and are in turn influenced by it.

Conservative Judaism in its various expressions, however, is not content with determining the constancy of certain ideas that possess universal significance. It is interested also in establishing a special Jewish corpus and holds that Jews must promote and foster their own peculiar possessions and norms. The preservation of the synagogue is thus made a constant factor in the life of Jews. Conservative Judaism also confers a definite status on various commandments.[2] Tradition is conceived not only as a summary of changes but also as a system of guiding principles that are constant. The normative status of the commandments (*mitzvot*) has its roots in a system of Jewish beliefs and opinions, but it is also justified with respect to the preservation of the Jewish community. Leaving aside the question of its ultimate value, a particular commandment may be honored for its antiquity—because it has worked, because it has been a cohesive factor in Jewish life, or because it has contributed to the creation of a style of life. It may be said that, whereas tradition once had a normative status by virtue of its content, it has now acquired, among other things, the status of an instrumental norm.[3]

THE MOVEMENTS DISCUSSED ABOVE regard themselves as religious and view the concept of tradition from different religious standpoints. But in describing the responses to the reinterpretation of tradition as dynamic, we must also attend to those movements which are not primarily religious, such as Zionism, Yiddishism and basically secular movements.

What all of these movements have in common is the goal of preserving the Jewish people as an ethnic, historical entity under modern conditions. These conditions, in our present context, may be approached in two ways: either in terms of the relationship between Jews and their political, social and cultural environment, or in terms of the continued existence of the Jewish people. The non-religious movements see an inner problem concerning the persistence of the Jewish people and its relation to its historic past. They do not regard tradition as a norm, nor do they consider it a vital factor that is part of some abstract system of thought, as does modern Reform Judaism. In contrast to the dynamic interpretation of tradition, these movements propound what may be called the idea of tradition as cumulative.

Within the tradition, they proclaim, there is room for various movements, ideas and basic religious beliefs. The elements they hold necessary for the preservation of the Jewish people in the present world are similar to those considered to be necessary by other national, rather than religious, cultures.

Foremost among these elements is a recognition of ties to Jewish history, though not in the sense of adherence to concepts of the past and religious modes of conduct of the past. The connection to the norms of tradition is superseded by a consciousness of the present, which though different from the past is nevertheless to be considered its continuation—at least from the standpoint of efforts to preserve the Jewish people as a national entity.

Insofar as it represents a national past, Jewish history deserves to be upheld in the present in much the same way that, say, European nations value their history. These nations do not regard their past as having inflexibly determined their customs and beliefs, but still see their contemporary existence as stemming from the works of preceding generations. Thus they honor their past without observing what they consider its obsolete forms and turn to it as their heritage and because it contains treasures worthy to be studied and known.

In the same spirit, these peoples study their own language not only as a medium of communication but also as a creative instrument through their cultural stages. They preserve their own thought, history and literature and assign these authentically national subjects a special place in the curriculum of their schools. A Jew traditionally studies the Talmud not in order to acquaint himself with the world of his fathers, but to familiarize himself with a document that has normative meaning for him here and now. But it is possible for a student of the Talmud to approach it as a document of the past; then he proceeds like a

Chaucer scholar or like a student of the history of French grammar—with no necessary sense of attachment to its values.

There is, however, another aspect of the non-religious
movements that is worth noting in relation to tradition in its
dynamic sense; that is, they all select and identify themselves
with particular, constant elements from the body of tradition,
elements which are not religious or ethical ideas proper. Thus
Zionism, in its more comprehensive sense, chooses the relationship of the Jewish people to the Land of Israel as one constant
factor in Jewish life throughout the ages and, as another, the
people's relation to the Hebrew language. Now, these two elements occupy a central position within the world of Jewish
tradition. Even the Reform Movement, which as we have noted
endeavored to reduce Judaism to its basic ideals, regarded these
elements as essential components of the tradition. But the
Zionists were inclined to view them not only as ideals but as
programs capable of being realized—as feasible norms for the
present day.

The same rationale applies *mutatis mutandis* to the Yiddishist
Movement or to the Jewish Workers Movement. For these,
Yiddish is the central, decisive element in the determination of
the ethnic-cultural identity of the Jewish people. The choice of
the Yiddish language is also of a methodological significance.
Yiddish was not the language of the forefathers but was acquired
late, when Jews entered the cultural world of Germany. However,
it became the language of many Jews and, in the course of
centuries, the medium of Jewish expression and creation. Its
historical roots went down deep enough so that it could be
considered a part of the national culture, an element of the
dynamic, historical experience of the Jews. Within this experience
—despite the fact that Yiddish was not accorded the historical
status granted Hebrew—it had sufficient prestige and impact to
constitute a factor of historical continuity that was, and seemed
likely to continue to be, unaffected by those processes which
alter the cultural image of Jewry.

THE VARIOUS APPROACHES TO TRADITION discussed above have one aspect in common: a relationship to tradition *qua* tradition. They seek to discover in tradition definite elements of content— whether that content be one of ideas, *mitzvot* or national survival—which can have normative value for the present day. But there is another approach to tradition that is not explicit in such ideological and popular movements as we have already considered.

The modern period of great scientific and technological achievement has been characterized by a tendency among individuals and people throughout the world to obliterate the differences between historical cultures and to create homogeneous patterns of life, including beliefs and opinions that are held in common by all men. But we know also that modern man lives on various levels at the same time. While he experiences existence on the level of a scientific culture that tends to universalism, he is not only an anonymous member of a world community, but a being who also leads—or may lead—a rich and varied life in more private areas. He is involved in particular relationships, and he is attached to what Erich Neumann in his dispute with Freud called the father factor. Partly, if not wholly, he resides within a historical culture or in certain areas of it.

Now a historical culture is not universalistic, and its peculiar contribution to the process of human history consists in this differentiating aspect. Just as an artificial language may be invented to serve the end of universal communication and yet not replace the national languages used in everyday life and in literary creation, so the historical culture persists along with the universalism of science. In the intimate circle of the family a historical language, not Esperanto, is spoken. So modern man is also a particular, historical being, attached to partial and fragmentary interests and perspectives.

The nature of this attachment may be described as existential, to distinguish it from attachments formed in accordance with material or substantive decisions, although its content may be very much the same. Thus, for a Jew, the existential decision can lead to an attachment to particular ideas derived from Jewish tradition, or to the Hebrew language and the Land of Israel, or to the whole tradition as one of the various historical traditions or even as one of the basic traditions that have deeply influenced Western culture. But there is an important difference between substantive and existential attachments. The former are *ab origine* relationships; that is, they are binding by reason of their origin. The latter are *post factum* relationships, likely to be formed out of feeling or sentiment or even practical considerations.

We have looked at ways in which the modern Jew—the Jew who affirms the world beyond the scope of Judaic norms—approaches the problem of his loyalty to his own traditions and to the preservation of his ethnic and cultural existence. We may now extend the scope of our inquiry and raise more comprehensive questions based on the assumption that Judaism is a historical, cultural and spiritual entity. Namely: Is there room in the modern world for a spiritual heritage that is consciously separate and might even be regarded as separatistic? And can we go beyond a discussion of a given consolidated tradition and consider certain basic assumptions of Judaism throughout the centuries which bear on the problems that beset men today?

IN A GENERAL WAY, we are forced to return to the question raised at the beginning of this book: what is the meaning of the concept of tradition? And the answer, finally, must be that tradition comprises the beliefs, opinions and ways of life observed by people here and now. In tradition there is a close relationship between man as he thinks and lives in the present and man as he thought and lived in the past, and it is obvious that between them there must be an enduring system of belief and a fixed code of conduct. A tradition is an impossibility for someone

who maintains that all is in a state of flux. Thus in any attachment
to the idea of tradition there is an element of what we may call
conservatism, for to hold to the past is to preserve it and to be
wary of change. Conservatism is disposed to cling to ideas and
ways not because of their intrinsic value, although it is prepared
to defend their value, but because of their age and status in the
past.

The intellectual and social world of Judaism is a world of
tradition, and the dilemma of the modern Jew is based on this
reality. Is he obligated to preserve Judaism and its tradition as
creations of the venerated past, that is, for conservative reasons,
or by reason of his appreciation of their content?

In approaching this question we must consider an instructive
fact—although it tends to deepen the dilemma—that the Jewish
tradition as an aggregate of ideas and regulations has been set
forth in the *Halakhah* and not in the Bible. There is of course a
connection, with which we shall deal later, between the Bible
and the *Halakhah*. But such Biblical ideas as those of creation,
the judgment and guidance of history, justice and the like, do not
themselves create a tradition of fixed and permanent regulations.
Such a tradition grows out of the encounter between general
rules and their expression in concrete situations.

The Bible is based on the idea that man is a responsible being
and as such is judged by God Who created man in His image.
Furthermore, because he is a thinking being, man is called upon
to account for his actions. The Judaic conception of man and
his responsibility is here different from that of Christianity on
the one hand and Islam on the other. We may say that it is only
by means of a conception which views man as answerable for
his deeds that we are able to arrive at the basic idea of *Halakhah*
and to reach the conclusions derived from this idea that constitute
the *Halakhah*. The *Halakhah* is connected to the Bible not only
from the literary-exegetical point of view, since the *Halakhah*
regards the Bible (or in the traditional formula, the Torah given
to Moses on Sinai) as its authority, but also because the *Halakhah*
attempts to determine the system of fixed, specifically defined

norms according to which man is to be judged. If he does one thing he will be punished in accordance with his guilt, and if he does another he will be rewarded in accordance with his merit. The normative force of the *Halakhah* lies in its assumption that man is called upon to follow certain paths in conformity with a summons directed to him. The *Halakhah* specifies the content of this summons. The idea that man is summoned is one that the *Halakhah* derived from the Bible but which it invested with obligation and interpreted in concrete ways.

There are, however, aspects of the transition from general principles to particular definitions and precepts that are problematical for *Halakhah*. The process of concretization has no limits. The idea of justice, for example, in itself offers no basis for deepening and expansion by establishing the specific Jewish conditions under which justice may be said to reside. But it is imperative that justice should be realized within the realm of the concrete; therefore the *Halakhah* sets up rules for the giving of charity to the poor, the codes and procedures to be followed by courts in interpreting the law and similar matters. But it is always possible to increase the number of regulations, since every situation is peculiar and every human action lends itself to detailed characterization. The *Halakhah* attempts to regulate private life in its physical, biological and spiritual aspects as well as the relations of man to his fellow man, to the community and to God. Concerned with particulars, it involves the Jew in a web of detailed prescriptions derived from the norm which may divert his attention from the basic meaning of *Halakhah*. Every thought or pattern of behavior has an existence of its own, and its meaning can be distorted when it is regarded in terms of its fundamental ideas alone. Broken down into detailed rules and instructions, it presents a danger of petrification, for then there may be a blurring of the relation between the particular instance and the general idea, between the individual deed and the higher law that governs it.

A different kind of problem of the *Halakhah* is based on the fact that all particular acts occur in time. The manner and circumstances of men's lives undergo changes in time, but since the *Halakhah* derives its authority from timeless revelation and its formulation from situations in the past, it tends to render judgment of matters in the present according to patterns which are dated. The particularity of the *Halakhah* constrains it to regard (to take a simple example) the turning on of an electric light as work, and work is forbidden on the Sabbath according to the concept of work as defined in a time when electricity was unknown. Thus the *Halakhah* not only reduces general ideas to the particularities of human behavior, but it also turns such particularities—in this instance the work of starting a fire— into general norms.

Although such inner problems are of the greatest gravity, the *Halakhah*, as a system of norms of human conduct in all areas, remains the key to the solution of the crisis of modern Judaism. But this system of norms must be reformulated, in the light of its basic principles, if the *Halakhah* is to be affirmed as a living body of laws and should not become merely a historical relic. For the modern Jew will not indefinitely adhere to Judaism because of its antiquity, but will do so because it contains valuable ideas to which he can subscribe. A commitment of this kind is not a unique act of judgment made at a particular time but a never-ending process. Each individual Jew is required to shape his life so that he is responsible for his deeds in all spheres of his existence—in his private and social life, in his relations with the world at large, and to God as the ultimate Judge of the universe —and he will, therefore, subscribe only to norms which are consistent with his highest ideals, his intelligence and his knowledge. Even a secular Jew would not find it unreasonable to mold his life unceasingly in accordance with such norms. This idea of the *Halakhah* will find its own new expressions in the modern world. These new expressions may not be identical with some in the present-day *Halakhah*. But the tradition will be preserved and given new life even as it is changed.

A particular historical event of our own day—the creation and existence of a Jewish State, a political entity which did not exist during the many generations in which the *Halakhah* was formulated—points up an additional need for such change. As a factor in the preservation of Jewish unity, Israel has rendered the unifying force of the *Halakhah*, to a greater or lesser degree, superfluous. So more than ever in its history, the vitality and continuance of the *Halakhah* are dependent on the philosophical value of its ideas—including an acknowledgment of the topical and ideological status of Israel.

The first question that confronted modern Judaism was that of the normative value of tradition. We now see that the answer to this question entails a return to norms that are behind or above and beyond tradition. Such a return receives its impetus from the existence of tradition, but it does not require Jews to regard tradition as a closed and sealed book. From an adherence to new norms will arise a new tradition that will at the same time be a perpetuation and a transformation of the old, effecting a meeting between tradition and reality and being affected by that very meeting.

BUT THE TRADITION WE ARE TALKING ABOUT—old and new— has a religious basis, and the problem of the value of religion in the life of modern man has a decisive bearing on the survival of Jewish tradition in any form. The place of religion in the contemporary world differs from the one it occupied in the Middle Ages and after. To a large extent that place has been taken over by the culture of science, to whose concepts and world views modern man has shown a ready attraction. The fundamental struggle of any religious tradition or idea in modern times has not been with its counterpart in another religion but with its alternatives in the non-religious world of scientific thought.

The grave problem presented for religion by science must be

dealt with by anybody interested in preserving or building a religious tradition. This is not to say that science has to be put down; its important place in the world must be acknowledged. But at the same time its proper function must be understood. That function is to delineate relationships within reality; it is not, however, to explain reality itself. In the formulation of some modern philosophers, science is not able to tell us why there is a reality. Religion—specifically the monotheistic religions— offers one possible explanation. This is implied in the idea of creation, according to which reality is the work of God. Indeed, from the point of view of religion, reality is not an independent and self-enclosed sphere that can be defined in terms of its relations as, for example, energy can be defined as an aspect of matter. Reality as a whole cannot be comprehended from within. To be able to turn to the source of reality is no small thing to one who is not content to accept it merely as given. Perhaps most men do not wish to inquire into the matter, but such an inquiry has a logic and justification of its own which constitute the basis of the religious approach to the world. Modern science does not and cannot invalidate this approach; it can obscure it, it can divert inquiry away from it, but it cannot deprive it of its content or direction.

Similarly with respect to man. However science explains the evolution of the human species, it does not account for the fact that man is a thinking creature, a being who asks questions concerning his own development and the nature and origin of reality as a whole. Religion, on the other hand, does provide an answer, though one which does not pretend to be rational, for the simple reason that it is not based on the evidence of facts or data. The religious concept of human reason as emanating from divine reason or revelation exists on an altogether different plane from its evolutionary or genetic counterparts, but it is no less respectable for that. Yet religious speculation, including that of Judaism, must come to grips with the basic questions raised by man concerning himself and his world, if it is to sustain itself amid the competition of non-religious and anti-religious alternatives.

In this respect it is of paramount importance that religious thinking understand the peculiar character of modern atheism. The dictum, "If there is a God, how could I bear not to be God?" expresses it to succinct perfection. Modern atheism is based not only on doubt of God's existence or on the argument that God's existence cannot be demonstrated by rational means, but also in the view of God's existence as limiting man's expansion and autonomous power, as an impediment to his dominion over all the world. Modern Jewish thought must appreciate its confrontation with his kind of atheism, whether it appears in an intellectualized form or as an unformulated sentiment which nevertheless broadly influences human behavior.

No attachment to tradition can in and of itself be maintained actively and cultivated creatively in the modern world, and no attachment to tradition can be fostered by tradition itself. We live in a world in which decisions with respect to specific religious conceptions and traditions must be made under present-day conditions and by way of confrontation with real problems. Such decisions can no longer be taken on the basis of patterns of thought of the past. The modern man who still clings to religion implicitly affirms religious values, but this affirmation may lack vital significance in a life-context to which it is largely irrelevant.

In this respect, the position of Jewish thought is not different from that of religious thought in general. The question that concerns us, after all, is not strictly a Jewish question. Can we decide in favor of Jewish religious thought and tradition only after approving the religious approach in general? Or is there something special, even if not exclusive, which Judaism can offer?

THE SKEPTICISM concerning the normative value and validity of the Jewish tradition is in fact an aspect of the criticism directed against tradition in general. This criticism stems from the modern world view which encompasses two interrelated phenomena: modern science, which operates from intellectual hypotheses that apply to the data of sensibility; and the modern state, based on the idea of equal rights and obligations for all men, regardless of nationality or religion.

Tradition, whether regarded from the viewpoint of science or the state, is conceived as a body of given beliefs and opinions that come from the past and are validated largely by their antiquity. Science proceeds on the assumption that man's understanding is not to be disturbed by his religious beliefs, whatever they may be, but yet will not hesitate to attack the latter—as we find in the criticism of Descartes and Bacon and even of a philosopher-believer like Pascal. The modern state in the formulation of its principles (as in the American Bill of Rights) assumes that the individual's relation to the world is unique and unmediated, and that this relation applies to all men who are born equal. His equality with his fellows defines each man's position as a citizen of his country, regardless of his adherence to any particular tradition.

The situation of the Jewish tradition as normative is, in this context, particularly acute, because Judaism presupposes a world view different from, but parallel to, and even more comprehensive than, that of science and the state. Leaving aside the question of the relative merits of each, the Jewish tradition has a value over and above its content: it has preserved the historic unity of the Jews throughout the generations and in every generation. Hence the attack on tradition is not only a peril to basic religious tenets but a destructive agent of national-historical significance.

Both modern science and the modern state tend to foster a style of life that follows universal principles which are not traditional. Today's Jew does not find himself removed from one tradition and placed within another (as, for example, that of Christianity), but thrust out of a mode of life that is traditional into one that is not, and which is continually extending itself and is continually being made anew. In the Middle Ages, Jewish thought was confronted with the ideas and traditions of Christianity and Islam, and its conflict was with these other systems of belief. Judaism, Christianity and Islam all offered themselves as bearers of eternal truths, and no small part of the efforts of medieval philosophers was devoted to the end of going beyond their limited particularities and demonstrating their universal or philosophic value. But this is different from what we find today. A particular system is not upheld or abandoned for the sake of universality. From the very outset we are immersed in a universalistic system, and even when this is not formulated on a conceptual, philosophic level, it is implicit in our daily culture. The ways we live and act are rooted in a scientific and egalitarian attitude to the world and thus also in a strictly human approach to man's social relations with his fellow man. Thus we find ourselves within a tradition which is not a tradition and from which it is unnecessary to depart in order to achieve a universal mode of life.

We have elsewhere alluded to the multi-level character of modern life—to sectors of existence which modern man shares with the generality of other men, and sectors in which he lives his private life. But there may be, and indeed there are, intermediate areas that are neither public nor private. A man is a member of a society, of a religion; a northern Italian is different from a southern Italian, an American from the Midwest may be distinguished from one from the South. And in such intermediate areas we also find the beliefs and ways representative of a particular ethnic or national tradition. Such a tradition, in some of its expressions, may be neutral with respect to the character of universal existence or, conversely, the latter may reconcile itself to the differences in the tradition. But the tradition—and this is particularly true of religious traditions such as Judaism—may take on value because it offers modes of response and conduct that are not available in the general sector.

A tradition contains symbolic elements inimical to the scientific or technological mode of life which, being based on a rational approach to the world, is naturally averse to symbolism. Such symbolic activity as the observance of traditional holy days and the celebrations at home in connection with them are deemed irrelevant to science, as is prayer. Science neither encourages nor opposes prayer, which has its origin in expectation and entreaty rather than in the interpretive approach of science to reality. Furthermore, if one wishes to maintain that the speculative side of Jewish tradition, which attempts to account for the structure of the world from a factual point of view, is not decisive, one might say that we are dealing with something larger than the scientific mode of life. The scientific mode of life does not in itself generate guidelines of conduct for man's relations to himself, to his fellow men or to the world. It may lead man to the full development of his intellectual powers without suggesting what he is to do with them or when he should employ them.

Here the moral content of a tradition such as Judaism may be of the most significant use in evaluating science and technology with respect to modern man, on the one hand, and in observing the limits of science and technology, on the other. Thus an attachment to such a tradition appears to be related to the general problem of modern culture. It may not be possible to escape from this culture; on the contrary, there is no choice but to refine and strengthen it, and some of the tools for this task lie in tradition. Science and tradition are not like two spheres existing side by side and mutually exclusive; each contains the possibility of a complementary relationship with the other, even though there is no complete harmony between them.

A TRADITION BASED ON IDEAS is faced with a special difficulty. Ideas tend to expand. Even when thought out by one individual they can be absorbed by another. When they are the product of a collective effort, they may pass from the group that originally

created them to another group or other groups. This is obviously
true of the ideas which comprise the Jewish tradition. To the
extent that this tradition is rooted in the Bible, it has also become
the property of general Western culture.

To give two instances: historical experience leads to a life
in accordance with religious and ethical imperatives; the widow
and the orphan are entitled to special consideration—these are
Biblical ideas which have become part of the general fabric of
ideas and been accepted both by the masses and their leaders.
Thus many Jews in our time are surprised to discover that the
Jewish tradition which they believed to be obsolete still has
meaning for them. While immersing themselves in the general
culture, they believe that they still, if indirectly, adhere to their
own tradition. To the extent that the one may be regarded as a
substitute for the other, the universality of traditional Jewish
ideas thus presents a grave danger to the tradition.

If he assumes that tradition has become a substantive part
of the culture of the non-Jewish world, the modern Jew is still
able to retain a special relationship to his tradition because of
the peculiar value of its source,* which non-Jews also recognize
as a factor in Jewish thought. The tradition may then be acknowledged as part of the general culture and as one of the material
sources of that culture. This was the position adopted by Hermann Cohen, who saw the rational character of the Jewish religion, and who also saw the religion of reason bound to the
historical and literary sources of Judaism.

But the adoption of this position immediately gives rise to
two important questions. Has the Jewish tradition really become
an integral part of Western culture or only certain parts of it?
And have these parts not suffered significant changes in the
process of becoming absorbed in the alien culture?

Let us take as an example one of the basic ideas of Judaism,
namely that God, the Creator of the universe, judges men's

---

* That is, the Bible and Jewish liturgy as well as Jewish medieval philosophy.

actions. There have been many interpretations of this idea. In the Christian polemics against Judaism it has been explained to mean that Judaism stresses justice to the exclusion of mercy. We need not in this context determine the correctness of this interpretation. But if we take the idea of man's responsibility to God based on God's overriding authority with respect to man, can we honestly say it is one of the ideas shared by Western culture? Insofar as it rests on the traditional view of God's nature and position vis-a-vis the world, the answer must be negative. Perhaps there is even a contradiction between the ideas of the culture of the environment and those that govern the Jewish tradition. In the former there is a tendency—which is an aspect of its scientific and technological character—not to judge man on the basis of his ability to do one thing or another, except within the limits of his capability as determined by scientific knowledge. Jewish tradition, on the other hand, tends to regard the limits of a man's actions as being independent of his capabilities, and as defined by imperatives imposed on him by his sense of responsibility. This is a very basic difference between the conceptual world of Judaism and that of Western culture.

Perhaps what we have here is an opposition between the conceptual worlds of religion in general and secular culture; but in the case of Judaism this opposition will be found to be most severe. In this light, no Jew can really argue that his tradition in its core has become a part of the general culture. He is bound to acknowledge that the reverse is true, and that he must spend his life choosing between ideas and tendencies which are contradictory. He cannot solve the problem simply by adopting an attitude of quietism.

The Jew can, of course, reject the conceptual world of Judaism altogether and look upon himself as a full citizen of the Western world. But if he does so, he no longer has the right to argue that his attachment to Western culture is at the same time an allegiance to Jewish tradition. The Jew who advocates the complete assimilation of Judaism into Western culture is bound to acknowledge the contradictory fact that such an assimilation is not taking place, and thus the argument that it has taken place is no solution to the problem.

This leads us finally to consider what may be the decisive elements in the Jewish tradition. For adherence to the tradition in times of crises cannot arise from the norm of the tradition itself. We must return to the basic ideas from which tradition arose and from which a coherent philosophy may be evolved.

The idea of man as subject to divine judgment in his relation to God the Creator, Who is at the same time the Judge of the universe, may well serve as the nucleus for such a philosophy. One can envisage different renderings of this idea, including some that may not sound religious at all. But no interpretation that fails to distinguish between core and shell is likely to prove satisfactory.

The progressive erosion of tradition as the norm in Jewish life, articulated by trends in Jewish thought, has reached its end. We can only return to primary concepts: the position of tradition in human life as against the contemporary tendency to live in the present even at the expense of the future. Here Jewish thought has to face what might be called the anthropological problem of tradition in human life.

And again not only in terms of the idea of tradition, but in terms of the validity of substantive ideas, Judaism has but one alternative: to attempt to reformulate some of the basic notions of the world outlook expressed in Judaic sources. Here, too, man and history might be the main issue and, to paraphrase an ancient Talmudic adage, everything else is but commentary.

NOTES

INTRODUCTION

1 Leo Steinberg, Excerpts from Conference II, *Daedalus,* Summer 1969, p. 792.

2 On the philosophical systems of these thinkers, see the present author's *From Mendelssohn to Rosenzweig, Jewish Philosophy in Modern Times* (New York, 1968).

CHAPTER ONE

1 In his *Philosophie der Geschichte, oder Über die Tradition* (Frankfurt a. M., 1827), I, p. 18.

2 See A. Zifroni's edition of *Sefer Hovath Ha-Levavoth* (The Duties of the Heart) (Jerusalem, 1928), p. 7.

3 *Das Judentum und seine Geschichte* (Breslau, 1865–1871), I, pp. 74 ff. (English: *Judaism and Its History,* tr. Ch. Newburgh, New York, 1911, I, pp. 86 ff.).

4 See S. Formstecher, *Die Religion des Geistes, eine wissenschaftliche Darstellung des Judenthums nach seinem Charakter, Entwicklungsgange und Berufe in der Menschheit* (Frankfurt a. M., 1841), pp. 87, 199, 201.

5 Consult the profound analysis in his "Offenbarung und Tradition als religiöse Kategorien im Judentum," *Über einige Grundbegriffe des Judentums,* Frankfurt a.M., 1970; pp. 90 ff.

6 A. Deneffe, S.J., *Der Traditionsbegriff, Studie zur Theologie* (Münster in Westph., 1931), p. 115.

7 H. Cohen, *Die Religion der Vernunft aus den Quellen des Judentums* (Leipzig, 1919), pp. 82 ff.

8 F. Scheiermacher, *Über die Religion, Reden an die Gebildeten unter ihren Verächtern* (Leipzig, 1920), pp. 110 ff. (English: *On Religion, Speeches to Its Cultured Despisers*, tr. J. Oman, New York, 1955, pp. 103 ff.)

9 See the present author's *Between Past and Present: An Essay on History* (New Haven, Conn., 1958), pp. 20–21.

CHAPTER TWO

1 L. Zunz, *Gesammelte Schriften* (Berlin, 1875), I, p. 5.

2 *Ibid.*, p. 4.

3 *Ibid.*, p. 57.

4 *Ibid.*

5 On the non-romantic element in Zunz's views see Ch. Steinthal, *Über Juden und Judentum. Vorträge und Aufsätze*, ed. G. Karpeles (Berlin, 1906).

6 Geiger pointed out this difference between the Science of Judaism and the Historical School. See "Eine Erinnerung an frühere Zeiten (Glückwunsch-schreiben an Herrn Dr. L. Zunz in Berlin zur Vollendung des siebzigsten Jahre am 10. August 1863)," in *Abraham Geigers Nachgelassene Schriften*, ed. L. Geiger (Berlin-London, 1875–1878), I. On the attitude towards the Historical School see F. Bamberger, "Zunz's Conception of History. A Study of the Philosophic Elements in Early Science of Judaism," *Proceedings of the American Academy for Jewish Research* XI (New York, 1941), pp. 1 ff.

7 See I. M. Jost, *Geschichte der Israeliten seit der Zeit der Maccabäer bis auf unsere Tage* (Berlin, 1820–1847), I, p. 8. See also I. Wolff, "Über den Begriff einer Wissenschaft des Judenthums," *Zeitschrift für die Wissenschaft des Judentums*, ed. L. Zunz, I/1 (Berlin, 1822), p. 15.

8 Zunz, *Gesammelte Schriften*, I, p. 134; I. Wolff, *op. cit.*, p. 18.

9 *Gesammelte Schriften*, I, p. 100.

10 *Ibid.*, p. 7.

11 *Ibid.*, pp. 134–141.

12 I. Wolff, *op. cit.*, pp. 4 ff.

13 S. L. Steinheim, *Die Offenbarung nach dem Lehrbegriffe der Synagoge* (Frankfurt a. M., 1835–1865), I, p. 26.

14 *Ibid.*

15 *Ibid.*, p. 29: "*Wir* entwickeln nicht *sie*; sondern *sie uns.*"

16 *Ibid.*, pp. 32–33.

17 Wolff, *op. cit.*, p. 6.

18 B. Z. Dinaburg (Dinur), *Israel Ba-Golah* (Israel in the Diaspora),

the fifth volume of his extensive history of Israel (Tel Aviv, 1925/
1926), pp. 14 ff.

19 *Ibid.*, p. 15.
20 *Gesammelte Schriften*, I, p. 101.
21 Zunz, *Nachtrag zur Literaturgeschichte der synagogalen Poesie*
(Berlin, 1867), p. 26.
22 *Gesammelte Schriften*, I, pp. 6, 7.
23 *Ibid.*, p. 99.
24 *Ibid.*, p. 42.
25 Wolff, *op. cit.*, p. 1.
26 Zunz, *Gesammelte Schriften*, I, p. 42 f.
27 *Ibid.*
28 *Ibid.* Consult S. Ucko, "Geistesgeschichtliche Grundlagen der
Wissenschaft des Judentums (Motive des Kulturvereins vom
Jahre 1819)," *Zeitschrift für die Geschichte der Juden in Deutsch-
land*, V. Jahrgang (Berlin, 1935), pp. 1–34.
29 Zunz, *Die gottesdienstlichen Vorträge der Juden*, p. 448.
30 *Idem, Gesammelte Schriften*, I, p. 42.
31 F. Bamberger, "Zunz's Conception of History. A Study of the
Philosophic Elements in Early Science of Judaism," *Proceedings
of the American Academy for Jewish Research* XI (New York, 1941),
pp. 1 ff.
32 "Über die Aufgabe des Geschichtsschreibers (1821)," in *Wilhelm
von Humboldts Ausgewählte philosophische Schriften*, ed. J. Schubert
(Leipzig, n.d.), pp. 81, 85, 89. The traces of von Humboldt's view
can be found in Zunz's writings.
33 I. Wolff, *op. cit.*, p. 24.
34 The address of Gans was published with an Introduction by
Zalman Rubaschoff, the now President of the State of Israel,
Zalman Shazar. See "Erstlinge. Einleitung zu den drei Reden von
Eduard Gans im Kulturverein," *Der Jüdische Wille* I (Berlin,
1918–1919), pp. 30 ff.
35 Zunz, *Gesammelte Schriften*, I, p. 53.
36 *Ibid.*
37 Wolff, *op. cit.*, p. 23.
38 On the critical evaluation of the Science of Judaism consult Gershom
G. Scholem, "Wissenschaft vom Judentum einst und jetzt," in
Judaica (Frankfurt a. M., 1963), pp. 147–164.

CHAPTER THREE

1 On the philosophical position of Krochmal, apart from his histor-
ico-philosophical view, see the present author's book, *From
Mendelssohn to Rozenzweig, Jewish Philosophy in Modern Time*
(New York, 1968), pp. 136 ff.

2 *Moreh Nevuhei Ha-zeman* (*Guide for the Perplexed of the Time*), incl. in *Kitvey Rabbi Nachman Krochmal,* ed. Sh. Rawidowicz (Berlin, 1924), p. 247. The references in parentheses are to this edition.

3 See the chapter on Krochmal in J. Guttmann, *Philosophies of Judaism, The History of Jewish Philosophers from Biblical Times to Franz Rosenzweig,* tr. D. W. Silverman (New York, 1966), pp. 365 ff.

4 J. G. Herder, *Ideen zur Philosophie der Geschichte der Menschheit,* in *Herders Werke,* ed. H. Düntzer (Berlin, n. d.), Dritter Teil, Ch. XV.

5 See G. Scholem, *Major Trends in Jewish Mysticism* (Jerusalem, 1941), p. 175.

CHAPTER FOUR

1 J. Braniss (1792–1873) was professor of philosophy in Breslau.

2 H. Graetz, *Die Konstruktion der jüdischen Geschichte, Eine Skizze* (Berlin, 1936) (henceforth = *Die Konstruktion*) p. 7 (first published in 1846).

3 *Die Konstruktion,* pp. 19 ff.

4 Graetz, *Geschichte der Juden von der ältesten Zeiten bis auf die Gegenwart,* ed. M. Brann (Leipzig, n.d.), I, p. XXXI.

5 *Die Konstruktion,* pp. 20 ff.

6 *Geschichte der Juden,* ed. S. Horowitz (Leipzig, 1908), IV, pp. 1 ff.

7 *Die Konstruktion,* p. 18.

8 *Geschichte der Juden,* IV, p. 3; *Die Konstruktion,* pp. 18–21.

9 *Die Konstruktion,* p. 21.

10 *Geschichte der Juden,* IV, p. 3.

11 Hermann Cohen deals with Graetz's conception of Jewish history in *Graetzens Philosophie der jüdischen Geschiche,* incl. in *Jüdische Schriften* (Berlin, 1924), III, pp. 203 ff.

CHAPTER FIVE

1 See D. Z. Dinaburg, *Israel Ba-Golah* (Israel in the Diaspora), *ed. cit.* (above, Ch. II, n. 18), Part I, pp. 18 ff.

2 S. M. Dubnow, *Jewish History, An Essay in the Philosophy of History* (Philadelphia, 1927), pp. 3 ff.

3 See "The Doctrine of Jewish Nationalism," in *Nationalism and History, Essays on Old and New Judaism,* ed. K. S. Pinson (Philadelphia, 1958), pp. 76 ff.

4 In the Introduction to the Hebrew version of his History of the World-People (Tel Aviv, 1923), p. 1.

5 *Ibid.,* p. 3.

6 *Nationalism and History*, p. 76.
7 *Ibid.*, p. 86.
8 *Ibid.*, p. 99.
9 *Ibid.*, p. 186.
10 *Ibid.*, pp. 78, 137.

CHAPTER SIX

1 See "Jewish and Christian Ethics" in *Ahad Ha-am, Essays, Letters, Memoirs*, tr. and ed. L. Simon (Oxford, 1946), pp. 127 ff.
2 *Ibid.*, pp. 2 ff.
3 In the above work, under the heading "Judaism and Asceticism."
4 *Op. cit.*, p. 126.
5 *Ibid.*
6 *Ibid.*, p. 115.
7 H. Cohen, *Die Religion der Vernunft aus den Quellen des Judentums* (Leipzig, 1919), pp. 215 ff. Consult the present author's *Jewish Philosophy in Modern Times: From Mendelssohn to Rosenzweig* (New York, Chicago, San Francisco, 1968), pp. 66 ff.
8 Y. Kaufmann, "Yiqarei Deotav shel Ahad Ha-am" (The Basic Principles of Ahad Ha-am), *Hatekufah* XXIV (Warsaw, 1928), pp. 421 ff.

CHAPTER SEVEN

1 *Devarim Shebe'al Peh* (Tel Aviv, 1935), p. 176.
2 *Ibid.*, p. 201.
3 *Ibid.*, p. 177.
4 *Ibid.*, p. 52.
5 *Ibid.*, II, p. 144.
6 *Ibid.*, p. 165.
7 *Ibid.*, p. 167.
8 *Ibid.*, p. 165.
9 *Ibid.*, p. 171.
10 *Ibid.*, I, p. 15.
11 *Ibid.*, II, p. 129.
12 *Ibid.*, I, p. 208.
13 *Ibid.*, p. 230.
14 *Ibid.*, p. 40.
15 *Ibid.*, p. 41.
16 *Ibid.*, p. 64.
17 *Ibid.*, p. 180.
18 *Ibid.*, p. 113.
19 *Ibid.*, p. 66.
20 *Collected Works* (Tel Aviv, 1953), II, p. 24.

21   *Devarim*, I, p. 186.
22   *Ibid.*, p. 202.
23   *Ibid.*, p. 200.

CHAPTER EIGHT

1   *Neunzehn Briefe über Judentum* (first published in 1836). (English: *Nineteen Letters of Ben Uziel; Being a Spiritual Presentation of the Principles of Judaism*, tr. B. Drachman, New York, 1942).
2   Consult: M. Davis, *The Emergence of Conservative Judaism, The Historical School in 19th Century America* (The Jewish Publication Society of America, Philadelphia, 1963–5723), pp. 283 ff. On its differences from the Reform Movement, *ibid.*, pp. 11–14.
3   Emancipation gave birth to many internal and external controversies. For a comment on one of these aspects, see present author's "For and Against Emancipation: The Bruno Bauer Controversy," *Leo Baeck Institute Year Book*, IV (London, 1959), pp. 3 ff. The present author dealt with the present-day climate of opinion in his *Humanism in the Contemporary Era*. The Hague, 1963.

GLOSSARY OF CONCEPTS
AND HISTORICAL TERMS

Cabbalists—Proponents of the mystic teachings of the "Cabbalah" (literally, "tradition").

Derekh Eretz—Good behavior, deportment, in the sense of following the rules pertaining to one's actions in worldly affairs.

Ecstatic (solution)—Characterized by an exalted state of feeling to the exclusion of rational thought.

Essenes—A body of pre-Christian Jews who lived a monastic life with community of property, practicing charity and hospitality, and observing a strict daily routine of prayers and work. The Essenes believed in the immortality of the soul and in a rigid determinism, condemned slavery and animal sacrifices, and thus placed themselves in opposition to the Jewish ritual life of their time.

German Historical School—A school of thought which regarded law as a historical product and not merely an expression of political will. Accordingly, law was to be identified with custom, tradition and the *Volksgeist* or genius particular to a nation or people. The school was founded by Savigny (1779–1861), influenced by Herder (1744–1803), Burke (1729–1797) and Hegel's conception of the spirit.

Halakhah (literally, "way to walk")—In contrast to *Haggadah* ("tale," "narrative"), the legal part of Jewish tradition, codified by Rabbi Judah ha-Nasi (135–c. 220) and comprising the juridical body of the Talmud and the later commentators.

Haskalah (literally, "cognition")—A movement in Eastern European Jewry towards Enlightenment which began in the early nineteenth century and which sought to infuse traditional Judaism with

modern cultural ideas. Inspired by the thought of Moses Mendelssohn, the movement spread via Austrian Galicia into both Russia
and Poland.

Massoret—from *Masorah,* the system of critical notes on the external
form of the Biblical text, representing the literary labors of innumerable scholars, beginning probably in pre-Maccabean times.
The original meaning of the word was "fetter" (suggesting the idea
of fixation of the text, the placing of a fetter on changes); later
Masorah assumed the sense of "tradition that was handed down."

Pharisees (literally, "separatists")—An ancient Hebrew party which
is believed to have become a sect in reaction to the attempt of
Antiochus Epiphanes (2nd century B.C.) to eliminate the distinction between Jews and Greeks. The Pharisees believed in oral law
to explain the Torah, in the immortality of the soul, and in the
resurrection of the dead. They insisted on a strict observance of
the law, developing a system of hermeneutics whose major rules
were formulated by Hillel (fl. 30 B.C.–A.D. 9).

Sadducees (probably "adherents of the Sons of Zadok")—A Jewish
sect or party of the last three centuries preceding the fall of Jerusalem (A.D. 70). According to Flavius Josephus, they did not
believe in fate nor in the immortality of the soul or resurrection,
emphasizing responsibility and free will. The Sadducees rejected
oral tradition and recognized only the authority of the written
law. Though as patriotic as the Pharisees, they were influenced by
Hellenism. Their adherents were typically the wealthy and the
aristocrats.

Shemitot (originally, "Sabbatical years")—A law or practice according
to which each seventh year the land was not to be sown, cultivated
or reaped and debts were to be remitted according to the Law of
Moses.

Talmud—Two works of the Palestinian and Babylonian schools of
the Amoraic period (3rd–5th centuries A.D.): the *Mishna* and the
Gemara. The *Mishna,* in Hebrew, is a systematic collection of
religious-legal decisions developing the laws of the Old Testament
(in contrast to the *Nigra* or scripture). The *Gemara,* in Aramaic
with Greek and Hebrew expressions, comprises an interpretation
and elaboration of the *Mishna.*

Sefer ha-Temunah or *Temunah* Book—A cabbalistic interpretation of
the evolution of the cosmos, according to which the secret content
of God reveals itself in various interpretations or phases and in
successive periods. Written c. 1250, the book first appeared in
print in 1784. Professor Gerschom Scholem regards it as an independent Jewish parallel to the theory of Joachim of Floris
(d. 1202), which posits three historical stages corresponding to the
three figures of the Christian Trinity.

Torah (literally, "doctrine")—The Pentateuch or Five Books of Moses (Genesis, Exodus, Leviticus, Numbers and Deuteronomy) considered as a single work, represented by the Scroll of the Law.

Yiddishism—A cultural movement which emerged in the twentieth century and whose aim it was to make the Yiddish language the basis of Jewish national identity and the core of the Jewish cultural renaissance. Polemically, Yiddishism took a negative position towards the revival of the Hebrew language as well as towards Zionism as a movement that denied the viability of the Diaspora, although there were Zionists who were culturally at home with Yiddish.

Zionism—A movement toward independence of the Jewish people in a publicly and legally assured home in Palestine. Political Zionism was initiated by Theodor Herzl in 1896.

INDEX

ABOUT THE AUTHOR

<small>NATHAN ROTENSTREICH</small> is Ahad Ha-am Professor of Philosophy
at the Hebrew University of Jerusalem. Born in Sambor, Poland,
in 1914, he emigrated to Palestine in 1932. He received his
M.A. and Ph.D. degrees from the Hebrew University,
and was a post-doctoral fellow at the University of Chicago.
Dr. Rotenstreich served as Principal of the Youth Aliyah
Teachers Training College from 1944 to 1951. In 1951
he became a member of the International Institute of
Philosophy and a member of the Israel Academy of Sciences
and Humanities. He was Rector of the Hebrew University
from 1963 to 1969. He was Visiting Professor at the Graduate
Center of City College, New York, 1969 to 1970 and
Visiting Fellow at the Center for the Study of Democratic
Institutions in Santa Barbara during the summer of 1970.

Professor Rotenstreich is the author of numerous
books and articles in both Hebrew and English, including
*Jewish Philosophy in Modern Times: From Mendelssohn
to Rosenzweig, The Recurring Pattern—Studies in
Anti-Judaism in Modern Thought,* and *Experience and
Its Systematization: Studies in Kant.* He is a co-translator,
with Professor S. H. Bergman, of Kant's three *Critiques*
into Hebrew.

Tradition and Reality is the third of a series of books
about modern Jewish civilization to be published by
Random House. Already published are *Flight and Rescue: Brichah,*
and *Israelis and Jews: The Continuity of an Identity.*
This series is under the general editorship of Dr. Moshe Davis,
head of the Institute of Contemporary Jewry, of the Hebrew
University of Jerusalem. The series is published with
the cooperation of the Institute.

DATE DUE

FEB 16 '80

GAYLORD			PRINTED IN U.S.A

DATE DUE

NOV 2 4 1995

NOV 3 0 1995

BM
195
.R84

19700
Rotenstreich, Nathan

Tradition and
reality

CHAMPLAIN COLLEGE LIBRARY

T 15810